Publications International, Ltd.

HERSHEY'S, MINI KISSES, MINICHIPS, REESE'S and SKOR are registered trademarks of Hershey Foods Corporation, Hershey, PA 17033. MOUNDS is a licensed trademark of Hershey Foods Corporation, Hershey, PA 17033.

All recipes developed and tested by the Hershey Kitchens.

Photographs on pages 19, 77 and 81 by William C. Simone, Simone Associates, Inc.

Photography: All photographs *except* those on pages 19, 77 and 81 by Photo/Kevin Smith.
Photographers: Kevin Smith, Greg Shapps
Photographers' Assistant: Jerry Cox
Prop Stylist: Erin Maxen
Food Stylists: Tobe LeMoine, Stephanie Samuels
Assistant Food Stylist: Vanessa Dubiel

Pictured on the front cover *(clockwise from right):* Deep Dark Chocolate Cake *(page 15),* Hershey's Buckeyes *(page 62),* Marbled Cheesecake Bars *(page 46),* Ultimate Chocolate Brownies with Creamy Cocoa Frosting *(page 41),* Mini Kisses Cookie Bars *(page 47)* and Bittersweet Truffle Toffee Mousse Pie *(page 85).*
Pictured on the back cover *(clockwise from top):* Crunchy-Topped Coffee Cake with Chocolatey Chips *(page 68),* Chocolatey Mocha Creme *(page 64)* Easy Chocolate Cream-Filled Torte *(page 78)* and Holiday Bits Cutout Cookies *(page 32).*

ISBN: 0-7853-3305-3

Manufactured in U.S.A.

8 7 6 5 4 3 2 1

Nutritional Analysis: Nutritional information is given for some of the recipes in this publication. Each analysis is based on the food items in the ingredient list. When more than one ingredient choice is listed, the first ingredient is used for analysis.

Microwave Cooking: Microwave ovens vary in wattage. Use the cooking times as guidelines and check for doneness before adding more time.

Prep/Bake Times: Prep times are based on the approximate amount of time required to assemble the recipe before baking, cooking, chilling or serving. These times include preparations steps such as measuring, chopping and mixing.

Contents

MIX IT UP WITH HERSHEY'S!   6

DELICIOUS CAKES   8

COOKIE JAR CLASSICS   22

BARS & BROWNIES   36

COLLECTION OF CANDY   52

THE LIGHTER SIDE   64

MEMORABLE DESSERTS   76

INDEX   93

Mix It Up With Hershey's!

Hershey's Best-Loved Recipes cookbook is devoted to chocolate lovers. The recipes featured are representative of our best chocolate recipes that you can make with the extensive line of Hershey's baking products that include:

Hershey's Cocoa—Classic, unsweetened, non-alkalized cocoa powder. Ideal for rich chocolate cakes, frostings, brownies, hot cocoa and other desserts.

Hershey's Dutch Processed Cocoa *European Style*—Unsweetened, alkalized cocoa powder with a dark reddish color and a unique, rich flavor for hot cocoa and special chocolate desserts.

Hershey's Semi-Sweet Chocolate Chips—Classic, deep, rich, semi-sweet chocolate.

Hershey's MiniChips Chocolate— A slightly smaller version of *Hershey's* Semi-Sweet Chocolate Chips with the same great taste. Ideal for muffins, cakes and pies.

Hershey's Milk Chocolate Chips—Creamy *Hershey's* milk chocolate.

Reese's Peanut Butter Chips—*Reese's* peanut butter taste in a chip.

Hershey's Premier White Chips—Delicious vanilla taste.

Hershey's Butterscotch Chips—Rich butterscotch flavor.

Hershey's Raspberry Chips—If you love chocolate and raspberry, you'll love these raspberry-flavored semi-sweet chocolate chips.

Hershey's Reduced Fat Baking Chips—Half the available fat of the traditional semi-sweet chips.

Hershey's Mini Kisses Chocolate—*Hershey's Kisses* Chocolates, but ⅓ the size. Unwrapped and ready to be poured into batter or used for a garnish. Available in both milk chocolate and semi-sweet.

Skor English Toffee Bits—The toffee center of a *Skor* candy bar broken into pieces perfect for baking and toppings.

Hershey's Baking Chocolate—Specially formulated, rich chocolate bars for baking in convenient 1 ounce pieces for great tasting chocolate desserts. Available in unsweetened, semi-sweet and bittersweet varieties.

Mounds Coconut—Moist, delicious, tender flaked coconut for baking and decorating.

Other products include *Reese's* Peanut Butter, *Hershey's* Mint Chocolate Chips, *Almond Joy* Coconut and Almond Bits, *Reese's* Peanut Butter Bits and *Hershey's* Holiday Bits.

With such a variety of products from which to choose, the possibilities are endless! We've included an index by recipe and product to make it easy for you to find the perfect recipe. Enjoy!

*D*elicious Cakes

TOFFEE BITS CHEESECAKE

CHOCOLATE CRUMB CRUST (recipe follows)
3 packages (8 ounces each) cream cheese, softened
¾ cup sugar
3 eggs
1¾ cups (10-ounce package) SKOR English Toffee Bits or 1¾ cups HEATH Bits 'O Brickle, divided
1 teaspoon vanilla extract
Sweetened whipped cream

1. Prepare CHOCOLATE CRUMB CRUST; set aside. Heat oven to 350°F.

2. Beat cream cheese and sugar in large bowl until smooth. Add eggs, one at a time, beating well after each addition. Set aside 1 tablespoon toffee bits. Gently stir remaining toffee bits and vanilla into batter; pour into prepared crust.

3. Bake 45 to 50 minutes or until almost set. Remove from oven to wire rack. With knife, loosen cake from side of pan. Cool completely; remove side of pan. Cover; refrigerate. Just before serving, garnish with sweetened whipped cream and reserved toffee bits. Cover; refrigerate leftover cheesecake.

10 to 12 servings

CHOCOLATE CRUMB CRUST: Heat oven to 350°F. Stir together 1¼ cups (about 40 wafers) vanilla wafer crumbs, ⅓ cup powdered sugar and ⅓ cup HERSHEY'S Cocoa in medium bowl; stir in ¼ cup (½ stick) melted butter or margarine. Press mixture firmly onto bottom and ½ inch up side of 9-inch springform pan. Bake 8 minutes; cool slightly.

PREP TIME: 25 minutes **BAKE TIME:** 45 minutes
COOL TIME: 1 hour **CHILL TIME:** 4 hours

Toffee Bits Cheesecake

CHOCOLATETOWN SPECIAL CAKE

½ cup HERSHEY'S Cocoa or HERSHEY'S Dutch Processed Cocoa
½ cup boiling water
⅔ cup shortening
1¾ cups sugar
1 teaspoon vanilla extract
2 eggs
2¼ cups all-purpose flour
1½ teaspoons baking soda
½ teaspoon salt
1⅓ cups buttermilk or sour milk*
ONE-BOWL BUTTERCREAM FROSTING (page 15)

To sour milk: Use 4 teaspoons white vinegar plus milk to equal 1⅓ cups.

1. Heat oven to 350°F. Grease and flour two 9-inch round baking pans.

2. Stir together cocoa and water in small bowl until smooth. Beat shortening, sugar and vanilla in large bowl until light and fluffy. Add eggs; beat well. Stir together flour, baking soda and salt; add to shortening mixture alternately with buttermilk, beating until well blended. Add cocoa mixture; beat well. Pour batter into prepared pans.

3. Bake 35 to 40 minutes or until wooden pick inserted in center comes out clean. Cool 10 minutes; remove from pans to wire racks. Cool completely. Frost with ONE-BOWL BUTTERCREAM FROSTING.

8 to 10 servings

PREP TIME: 30 minutes **BAKE TIME:** 35 minutes **COOL TIME:** 2 hours

PEANUT BUTTER CHIP CHEESECAKE

⅓ cup butter or margarine, melted
1¼ cups graham cracker crumbs
⅓ cup HERSHEY'S Cocoa
⅓ cup sugar
1 cup REESE'S Peanut Butter Chips
2 packages (8 ounces each) cream cheese, softened
1 can (14 ounces) sweetened condensed milk (not evaporated milk)
4 eggs
1 teaspoon vanilla extract
Whipped cream and chocolate curls or shavings (optional)

1. Heat oven to 300°F.

2. Stir together butter, crumbs, cocoa and sugar in medium bowl; press firmly on bottom of 9-inch springform pan or 13×9-inch baking pan.

3. Place peanut butter chips in small microwave-safe bowl. Microwave at HIGH (100%) 1 minute; stir. If necessary, microwave at HIGH an additional 15 seconds at a time, stirring after each heating, just until chips are melted when stirred. Meanwhile, beat cheese until fluffy. Gradually beat in sweetened condensed milk and melted chips until smooth. Add eggs and vanilla; mix well. Pour into prepared pan.

4. Bake 50 to 60 minutes or until cake springs back when touched lightly. Cool to room temperature. Refrigerate. Garnish with whipped cream and chocolate curls, if desired. Cover; refrigerate leftover cheesecake.

12 servings

PREP TIME: 30 minutes   **BAKE TIME:** 50 minutes   **COOL TIME:** 1 hour
CHILL TIME: 4 hours

CHOCOLATE TRUFFLE CAKE SUPREME

  1¼ **cups (2½ sticks) unsalted butter**
  ¾ **cup HERSHEY'S Cocoa**
  1 **cup plus 1 tablespoon sugar, divided**
  1 **tablespoon all-purpose flour**
  2 **teaspoons vanilla extract**
  4 **eggs, separated**
  1 **cup (½ pint) cold whipping cream**
    Chocolate curls (optional)

1. Heat oven to 425°F. Grease bottom of 8-inch springform pan. Melt butter in medium saucepan over low heat. Add cocoa and 1 cup sugar, stir well. Remove from heat; cool. Stir in flour and vanilla. Add egg yolks, one at a time, beating well after each addition. Beat egg whites in medium bowl with remaining 1 tablespoon sugar until soft peaks form; gradually fold into chocolate mixture. Spoon batter into pan.

2. Bake 16 to 18 minutes or until edges are firm (center will be soft). Cool completely on wire rack (cake will sink slightly in center as it cools). Remove side of pan. Refrigerate cake at least 6 hours.

3. Beat whipping cream in small bowl until soft peaks form; spread over top of cake. Cut cake while cold, but let stand at room temperature 10 to 15 minutes before serving. Garnish with chocolate curls, if desired.

10 servings

PREP TIME: 20 minutes   **BAKE TIME:** 16 minutes   **COOL TIME:** 1 hour
CHILL TIME: 6 hours

CHOCOLATE RASPBERRY POUND CAKE

    1 cup seedless black raspberry preserves, divided*
    2 cups all-purpose flour
 1½ cups granulated sugar
    ¾ cup HERSHEY'S Cocoa
 1½ teaspoons baking soda
    1 teaspoon salt
    ⅔ cup butter or margarine, softened
    1 container (16 ounces) dairy sour cream
    2 eggs
    1 teaspoon vanilla extract
      Powdered sugar
      RASPBERRY CREAM (recipe follows)

Red raspberry jam may be substituted.

1. Heat oven to 350°F. Grease and flour 12-cup fluted tube pan.

2. Place ¾ cup preserves in small microwave-safe bowl. Microwave at HIGH (100%) 30 to 45 seconds or until melted; cool. Stir together flour, granulated sugar, cocoa, baking soda and salt in large bowl. Add butter, sour cream, eggs, vanilla and melted preserves; beat on medium speed of electric mixer 3 to 4 minutes until well blended. Pour batter into prepared pan.

3. Bake 50 to 60 minutes or until wooden pick inserted in center comes out clean. Cool 10 minutes; remove from pan to wire rack. Place remaining ¼ cup preserves in small microwave-safe bowl. Microwave at HIGH 30 seconds or until melted; brush over warm cake. Cool completely.

4. At serving time, sprinkle powdered sugar over top. Prepare RASPBERRY CREAM; fill cavity with cream. Garnish, if desired.

About 12 servings

RASPBERRY CREAM: Thaw 1 package (10 ounces) frozen red raspberries in light syrup. Purée in food processor or blender. Strain into medium bowl; discard seeds. Blend 3½ cups (8 ounces) frozen non-dairy whipped topping, thawed, with raspberry purée. Stir in 2 tablespoons raspberry-flavored liqueur, if desired.

PREP TIME: 35 minutes   **BAKE TIME:** 50 minutes   **COOL TIME:** 3 hours

Chocolate Raspberry Pound Cake

QUICK 'N' EASY CHOCOLATE CUPCAKES

        2 cups all-purpose flour
    1½ cups sugar
        ⅔ cup HERSHEY'S Cocoa
        2 teaspoons baking powder
        ½ teaspoon baking soda
        ½ teaspoon salt
        ⅔ cup shortening
        2 eggs
        ⅔ cup milk
        ½ cup hot water
    1½ teaspoons vanilla extract
        CREAMY FUDGE FROSTING (recipe follows)

1. Heat oven to 350°F. Line muffin cups (2½ inches in diameter) with paper bake cups.

2. Stir together flour, sugar, cocoa, baking powder, baking soda and salt in large bowl. Add shortening, eggs, milk, water and vanilla; beat on low speed of electric mixer 1 minute. Beat on medium speed an additional 3 minutes or until mixture is smooth. Fill cups ½ full with batter.

3. Bake 15 to 20 minutes or until center of cupcake springs back when touched lightly in center. Remove cupcakes from pan to wire rack. Cool completely. (Do not cool cupcakes in pan; paper liners will come loose from cupcakes.)

4. Prepare CREAMY FUDGE FROSTING; frost cupcakes. Decorate, if desired. *About 30 cupcakes*

Creamy Fudge Frosting

        ½ cup (1 stick) butter or margarine
        ½ cup HERSHEY'S Cocoa
    3⅔ cups (1 pound) powdered sugar
    1½ teaspoons vanilla extract
        Dash salt
        ⅓ cup water

Melt butter in medium saucepan over low heat. Add cocoa; stir until smooth and well blended. Remove from heat. Add powdered sugar, vanilla and salt alternately with water; beat with spoon or whisk until smooth and creamy. Additional water may be added, ½ teaspoon at a time, if frosting becomes too thick. *About 2 cups frosting*

PREP TIME: 45 minutes   **BAKE TIME:** 15 minutes   **COOL TIME:** 1 hour

DEEP DARK CHOCOLATE CAKE

        2 cups sugar
    1¾ cups all-purpose flour
        ¾ cup HERSHEY'S Cocoa or HERSHEY'S Dutch Processed Cocoa
    1½ teaspoons baking powder
    1½ teaspoons baking soda
        1 teaspoon salt
        2 eggs
        1 cup milk
        ½ cup vegetable oil
        2 teaspoons vanilla extract
        1 cup boiling water
            ONE-BOWL BUTTERCREAM FROSTING (recipe follows)

1. Heat oven to 350°F. Grease and flour two 9-inch round baking pans or one 13×9×2-inch baking pan.

2. Stir together sugar, flour, cocoa, baking powder, baking soda and salt in large bowl. Add eggs, milk, oil and vanilla; beat on medium speed of electric mixer 2 minutes. Stir in boiling water (batter will be thin). Pour batter into prepared pans.

3. Bake 30 to 35 minutes for round pans, 35 to 40 minutes for rectangular pan or until wooden pick inserted in center comes out clean. Cool 10 minutes; remove from pans to wire racks. Cool completely. (Cake may be left in rectangular pan, if desired.)

4. Prepare ONE–BOWL BUTTERCREAM FROSTING; frost cake.

8 to 10 servings

One-Bowl Buttercream Frosting

        6 tablespoons butter or margarine, softened
    2⅔ cups powdered sugar
        ½ cup HERSHEY'S Cocoa or HERSHEY'S Dutch Processed Cocoa
        4 to 6 tablespoons milk
        1 teaspoon vanilla extract

Beat butter in medium bowl. Add powdered sugar and cocoa alternately with milk, beating to spreading consistency. Stir in vanilla.

About 2 cups frosting

PREP TIME: 20 minutes   **BAKE TIME:** 30 minutes   **COOL TIME:** 2 hours

CRUNCHY–TOPPED COCOA CAKE

> ### TIP
> *To make a single serving of "Perfectly Chocolate" Hot Cocoa, stir 2 tablespoons sugar, 2 teaspoons Hershey's Cocoa and a dash of salt in large microwave-safe mug. Gradually add 1 cup hot milk and 1/4 teaspoon vanilla extract, stirring until well blended. Top with miniature marsh-mallows, if desired.*

1½ cups all-purpose flour
 1 cup sugar
¼ cup HERSHEY'S Cocoa
 1 teaspoon baking soda
½ teaspoon salt
 1 cup water
¼ cup plus 2 tablespoons vegetable oil
 1 tablespoon white vinegar
 1 teaspoon vanilla extract
 BROILED TOPPING (recipe follows)

1. Heat oven to 350°F. Grease and flour 8-inch square baking pan.

2. Stir together flour, sugar, cocoa, baking soda and salt in large bowl. Add water, oil, vinegar and vanilla; beat with spoon or whisk just until batter is smooth and ingredients are well blended. Pour batter into prepared pan.

3. Bake 35 to 40 minutes or until wooden pick inserted in center comes out clean. Meanwhile, prepare BROILED TOPPING; spread on warm cake. Set oven to broil; place pan about 4 inches from heat. Broil 3 minutes or until top is bubbly and golden brown. Remove from oven. Cool completely in pan on wire rack.

9 servings

Broiled Topping

¼ cup (½ stick) butter or margarine, softened
½ cup packed light brown sugar
½ cup coarsely chopped nuts
½ cup MOUNDS Sweetened Coconut Flakes
 3 tablespoons light cream or evaporated milk

Stir together all ingredients in small bowl until well blended.

About 1 cup topping

PREP TIME: 20 minutes   **BAKE TIME:** 35 minutes
COOL TIME: 1½ hours

Crunchy-Topped Cocoa Cake

TAKE–ME–TO–A–PICNIC CAKE

      1 cup water
      1 cup (2 sticks) butter or margarine
    ½ cup HERSHEY'S Cocoa
      2 cups sugar
  1¾ cups all-purpose flour
      1 teaspoon baking soda
    ½ teaspoon salt
      3 eggs
    ¾ cup dairy sour cream
        PEANUT BUTTER CHIP FROSTING (recipe follows)
        CHOCOLATE GARNISH (optional, recipe follows)

1. Heat oven to 350°F. Grease and flour 15½×10½×1-inch jelly-roll pan. Combine water, butter and cocoa in medium saucepan. Cook over medium heat, stirring occasionally, until mixture boils. Boil 1 minute. Remove from heat. Stir together sugar, flour, baking soda and salt in large bowl. Add eggs and sour cream; beat until blended. Add cocoa mixture; beat just until blended. Pour into prepared pan.

2. Bake 25 to 30 minutes or until wooden pick inserted in center comes out clean. Cool on wire rack. Prepare PEANUT BUTTER CHIP FROSTING. Spread over cake. Prepare CHOCOLATE GARNISH; drizzle over top, if desired.   *About 20 servings*

PEANUT BUTTER CHIP FROSTING: Combine ⅓ cup butter or margarine, ⅓ cup milk and 1⅔ cups (10-ounce package) REESE'S Peanut Butter Chips in medium saucepan. Cook over low heat, stirring constantly, until chips are melted and mixture is smooth. Remove from heat; stir in 1 teaspoon vanilla extract. Place 1 cup powdered sugar in medium bowl. Gradually add chip mixture; beat well.   *About 2 cups frosting*

CHOCOLATE GARNISH: Place ½ cup HERSHEY'S Semi-Sweet Chocolate Chips and 1 teaspoon shortening (not butter, margarine or oil) in small microwave-safe bowl. Microwave at HIGH (100%) 1 minute; stir until chips are melted and mixture is smooth.

PREP TIME: 30 minutes   **BAKE TIME:** 25 minutes   **COOL TIME:** 1 hour

Take-Me-to-a-Picnic Cake

FUDGE TRUFFLE CHEESECAKE

CHOCOLATE CRUMB CRUST (recipe follows)
2 cups (12-ounce package) HERSHEY'S Semi-Sweet
    Chocolate Chips
3 packages (8 ounces each) cream cheese, softened
1 can (14 ounces) sweetened condensed milk (not
    evaporated milk)
4 eggs
2 teaspoons vanilla extract

1. Prepare CHOCOLATE CRUMB CRUST; set aside. Heat oven to 300°F.

2. Place chocolate chips in microwave-safe bowl. Microwave at HIGH (100%) 1½ minutes; stir. If necessary, microwave at HIGH an additional 15 seconds at a time, stirring after each heating, just until chips are melted when stirred.

3. Beat cream cheese in large bowl until fluffy. Gradually beat in sweetened condensed milk until smooth. Add melted chips, eggs and vanilla; mix well. Pour into prepared crust.

4. Bake 1 hour and 5 minutes or until center is set. Remove from oven to wire rack. With knife, loosen cake from side of pan. Cool completely; remove side of pan. Refrigerate several hours before serving. Garnish as desired. Cover; refrigerate leftover cheesecake. *10 to 12 servings*

CHOCOLATE CRUMB CRUST: Stir together 1½ cups vanilla wafer crumbs, ½ cup powdered sugar, ⅓ cup HERSHEY'S Cocoa and ⅓ cup melted butter or margarine in bowl. Press firmly onto bottom of 9-inch springform pan.

PREP TIME: 25 minutes   **BAKE TIME:** 1 hour 5 minutes
COOL TIME: 1½ hours   **CHILL TIME:** 4 hours

Fudge Truffle Cheesecake

HOLIDAY CHOCOLATE SHORTBREAD COOKIES

....

  1 cup (2 sticks) butter, softened
1¼ cups powdered sugar
  1 teaspoon vanilla extract
½ cup HERSHEY'S Dutch Processed Cocoa or HERSHEY'S Cocoa
1¾ cups all-purpose flour
1⅔ cups (10-ounce package) HERSHEY'S Premier White Chips

1. Heat oven to 300°F. Beat butter, powdered sugar and vanilla in large bowl until creamy. Add cocoa; beat until well blended. Gradually add flour, stirring until smooth.

2. Roll or pat dough to ¼-inch thickness on lightly floured surface or between 2 pieces of wax paper. Cut into holiday shapes using star, tree, wreath or other cookie cutters. Reroll dough scraps, cutting cookies until dough is used. Place on ungreased cookie sheet.

3. Bake 15 to 20 minutes or just until firm. Immediately place white chips, flat side down, in decorative design on warm cookies. Cool slightly; remove from cookie sheet to wire rack. Cool completely. Store in airtight container.

About 4½ dozen (2-inch diameter) cookies

NOTE: For more even baking, place similar shapes and sizes of cookies on same cookie sheet.

PREP TIME: 30 minutes   **BAKE TIME:** 15 minutes
COOL TIME: 30 minutes

Holiday Chocolate Shortbread Cookies

HERSHEY'S MINI KISSES PEANUT BLOSSOMS

½ cup shortening
¾ cup REESE'S Creamy Peanut Butter
⅓ cup granulated sugar
⅓ cup packed light brown sugar
1 egg
2 tablespoons milk
1 teaspoon vanilla extract
1½ cups all-purpose flour
1 teaspoon baking soda
½ teaspoon salt
Additional granulated sugar
1¾ cups (10-ounce package) HERSHEY'S MINI KISSES Chocolate

1. Heat oven to 375°F. Beat shortening and peanut butter in large bowl until well blended. Add ⅓ cup granulated sugar and brown sugar; beat until light and fluffy. Add egg, milk and vanilla; beat well.

2. Stir together flour, baking soda and salt; gradually add to peanut butter mixture, beating until well blended. Shape dough into 1-inch balls. Roll in additional granulated sugar; place on ungreased cookie sheet.

3. Bake 8 to 10 minutes or until lightly browned. Immediately place 3 MINI KISSES on top of each cookie, pressing down lightly. Remove from cookie sheet to wire rack. Cool completely.

About 4 dozen cookies

PREP TIME: 25 minutes   **BAKE TIME:** 8 minutes   **COOL TIME:** 1 hour

FUDGEY COCOA NO–BAKE TREATS

2 cups sugar
½ cup (1 stick) butter or margarine
½ cup milk
⅓ cup HERSHEY'S Cocoa
⅔ cup REESE'S Crunchy Peanut Butter
3 cups quick-cooking rolled oats
½ cup chopped peanuts (optional)
2 teaspoons vanilla extract

1. Place piece of wax paper or foil on tray or cookie sheet. Combine sugar, butter, milk and cocoa in medium saucepan.

2. Cook over medium heat, stirring constantly, until mixture comes to a rolling boil.

3. Remove from heat; cool 1 minute.

4. Add peanut butter, oats, peanuts, if desired, and vanilla; stir to mix well. Quickly drop mixture by heaping teaspoons onto wax paper or foil. Cool completely. Store in cool, dry place. *About 4 dozen*

PREP TIME: 20 minutes   **COOK TIME:** 5 minutes   **COOL TIME:** 30 minutes

HERSHEY'S MINI KISSES CHOCOLATE BLOSSOMS

   1 **cup (2 sticks) butter or margarine, softened**
1½ **cups sugar**
   2 **eggs**
   2 **teaspoons vanilla extract**
   2 **cups all-purpose flour**
 ½ **cup HERSHEY'S Cocoa**
 ½ **teaspoon salt**
   Additional sugar
1¾ **cups (10-ounce package) HERSHEY'S MINI KISSES Semi-Sweet Chocolate**

1. Beat butter, 1½ cups sugar, eggs and vanilla in large bowl until light and fluffy. Stir together flour, cocoa and salt; gradually add to butter mixture, beating until well blended.

2. Refrigerate dough about 1 hour or until firm enough to handle. Heat oven to 350°F. Shape dough into 1⅛-inch balls; roll in additional sugar. Place on ungreased cookie sheet.

3. Bake 8 to 10 minutes or until set. Place 3 MINI KISSES on top of each cookie, pressing down lightly. Remove from cookie sheet to wire rack. Cool completely. *About 4 dozen cookies*

PREP TIME: 25 minutes   **CHILL TIME:** 1 hour   **BAKE TIME:** 8 minutes
COOL TIME: 1 hour

FUDGEY GERMAN CHOCOLATE SANDWICH COOKIES

1¾ cups all-purpose flour
1½ cups sugar
¾ cup (1½ sticks) butter or margarine, softened
⅔ cup HERSHEY'S Cocoa or HERSHEY'S Dutch Processed Cocoa
¾ teaspoon baking soda
¼ teaspoon salt
2 eggs
2 tablespoons milk
1 teaspoon vanilla extract
½ cup finely chopped pecans
COCONUT AND PECAN FILLING (recipe follows)

1. Heat oven to 350°F. Stir together flour, sugar, butter, cocoa, baking soda and salt in large bowl. Add eggs, milk and vanilla; beat on medium speed of electric mixer until blended. Dough will be stiff. Stir in pecans.

2. Shape dough into 1¼-inch balls. Place on ungreased cookie sheet; flatten slightly.

3. Bake 9 to 11 minutes or until almost set. Cool slightly; remove from cookie sheet to wire rack. Cool completely. Prepare COCONUT AND PECAN FILLING. Put cookies together in pairs with about 1 heaping tablespoon filling for each cookie. Serve warm or at room temperature.

About 17 sandwich cookies

Coconut and Pecan Filling

½ cup (1 stick) butter or margarine
½ cup packed light brown sugar
¼ cup light corn syrup
1 cup MOUNDS Sweetened Coconut Flakes, toasted
1 cup finely chopped pecans
1 teaspoon vanilla extract

Melt butter in medium saucepan over medium heat; add brown sugar and corn syrup. Stir constantly until thick and bubbly. Remove from heat; stir in coconut, pecans and vanilla. Use warm. *About 2 cups filling*

PREP TIME: 25 minutes   **BAKE TIME:** 9 minutes   **COOL TIME:** 35 minutes

*Fudgey German Chocolate
Sandwich Cookies*

CHOCOLATE ALMOND BISCOTTI

½ cup (1 stick) butter or margarine, softened
1¼ cups sugar
2 eggs
1 teaspoon almond extract
2¼ cups all-purpose flour
¼ cup HERSHEY'S Dutch Processed Cocoa or HERSHEY'S Cocoa
1 teaspoon baking powder
¼ teaspoon salt
1 cup sliced almonds
CHOCOLATE GLAZE (recipe follows)
WHITE GLAZE (recipe follows)
Additional sliced almonds (optional)

1. Heat oven to 350°F. Beat butter and sugar until blended. Add eggs and almond extract; beat well. Stir together flour, cocoa, baking powder and salt; gradually add to butter mixture, beating until smooth. (Dough will be thick.) Stir in almonds using wooden spoon.

2. Shape dough into two 11-inch-long rolls. Place rolls 3 to 4 inches apart on large ungreased cookie sheet.

3. Bake 30 minutes or until rolls are set. Remove from oven; cool on cookie sheet 15 minutes. Using serrated knife, cut rolls diagonally using sawing motion, into ½-inch-thick slices. Arrange slices, cut sides down, close together on cookie sheet.

4. Bake 8 to 9 minutes. Turn slices over; bake an additional 8 to 9 minutes. Remove from oven; cool on cookie sheet on wire rack. Prepare CHOCOLATE GLAZE. Dip end of each biscotti in glaze or drizzle over entire cookie. Prepare WHITE GLAZE; drizzle over chocolate glaze. Garnish with additional almonds, if desired.   *About 2½ dozen cookies*

CHOCOLATE GLAZE: Place 1 cup HERSHEY'S Semi-Sweet Chocolate Chips and 1 tablespoon shortening (do not use butter, margarine or oil) into small microwave-safe bowl. Microwave at HIGH (100%) 1 to 1½ minutes or until smooth when stirred.   *About 1 cup glaze*

WHITE GLAZE: Place ¼ cup HERSHEY'S Premier White Chips and 1 teaspoon shortening (do not use butter, margarine or oil) into small microwave-safe bowl. Microwave at HIGH (100%) 30 to 45 seconds or until smooth when stirred.   *About ¼ cup glaze*

PREP TIME: 30 minutes   **BAKE TIME:** 46 minutes   **COOL TIME:** 1 hour

Chocolate Almond Biscotti

NO–BAKE BUTTERSCOTCH HAYSTACKS

  1 cup HERSHEY'S Butterscotch Chips
  ½ cup REESE'S Peanut Butter Chips
  1 tablespoon shortening (do not use butter, margarine or oil)
1½ cups (3-ounce can) chow mein noodles, coarsely broken

1. Line cookie sheet with wax paper. Place butterscotch chips, peanut butter chips and shortening in medium microwave-safe bowl.

2. Microwave at HIGH (100%) 1 minute; stir. If necessary, microwave at HIGH an additional 15 seconds at a time, stirring after each heating, just until chips are melted and mixture is smooth when stirred.

3. Immediately add chow mein noodles; stir to coat. Drop mixture by heaping teaspoons onto prepared cookie sheet or into paper candy cups; let stand until firm. If necessary, cover and refrigerate until firm. Store in refrigerator in tightly covered container.   *About 2 dozen cookies*

CHOCOLATE HAYSTACKS: Substitute 1 cup HERSHEY'S Semi-Sweet Chocolate Chips or HERSHEY'S Milk Chocolate Chips for butterscotch chips. Proceed as directed above with peanut butter chips, shortening and chow mein noodles.

PREP TIME: 15 minutes   **COOK TIME:** 1 minute   **COOL TIME:** 30 minutes

HERSHEY'S CHOCOLATETOWN CHIP COOKIES

  1 cup shortening OR ¾ cup (1½ sticks) butter or margarine
  1 cup packed light brown sugar
  ½ cup granulated sugar
  1 teaspoon vanilla extract
  2 eggs
2¼ cups all-purpose flour
  1 teaspoon baking soda
  1 teaspoon salt
  2 cups (11.5-ounce package) HERSHEY'S Milk Chocolate Chips
  1 cup chopped nuts (optional)

1. Heat oven to 375°F. Beat shortening, brown sugar, granulated sugar and vanilla in large bowl until light and fluffy. Add eggs; beat well.

2. Stir together flour, baking soda and salt; add to beaten mixture, stirring until well blended. Stir in chips and nuts, if desired. Drop by teaspoons onto ungreased cookie sheet.

3. Bake 8 to 10 minutes or until lightly browned. Cool slightly; remove from cookie sheet to wire rack. Cool completely.

About 5 dozen cookies

PREP TIME: 25 minutes   **BAKE TIME:** 8 minutes   **COOL TIME:** 35 minutes

SKOR BITS & CHOCOLATE CHIP COOKIES

2¼ cups all-purpose flour
1 teaspoon baking soda
½ teaspoon salt
¾ cup (1½ sticks) butter or margarine, softened
¾ cup granulated sugar
¾ cup packed light brown sugar
1 teaspoon vanilla extract
2 eggs
1 cup SKOR English Toffee Bits or 1 cup HEATH Bits 'O Brickle
1 cup HERSHEY'S Semi-Sweet Chocolate Chips

1. Heat oven to 375°F. Stir together flour, baking soda and salt. Beat butter, granulated sugar, brown sugar and vanilla in large bowl until well blended. Add eggs; beat well.

2. Gradually add flour mixture, beating well. Stir in toffee bits and chocolate chips. Drop dough by rounded teaspoons onto ungreased cookie sheet.

3. Bake 8 to 10 minutes or until lightly browned. Cool slightly; remove from cookie sheet to wire rack. Cool completely.

About 4 dozen cookies

PREP TIME: 25 minutes   **BAKE TIME:** 8 minutes   **COOL TIME:** 30 minutes

HOLIDAY BITS CUTOUT COOKIES

TIP

Brownies, bars and cookies make great gifts. Place them in a paper-lined tin or on a decorative plate covered with plastic wrap and tied with colorful ribbon. For a special touch, include the recipe.

1 cup (2 sticks) butter or margarine, softened
1 cup sugar
2 eggs
2 teaspoons vanilla extract
2½ cups all-purpose flour
½ teaspoon baking powder
½ teaspoon salt
HERSHEY'S Holiday Candy Coated Bits

1. Beat butter, sugar, eggs and vanilla in large bowl on low speed of electric mixer just until blended. Stir together flour, baking powder and salt; add to butter mixture, stirring until well blended.

2. Divide dough in half. Cover; refrigerate 1 to 2 hours or until firm enough to handle. Heat oven to 400°F. On lightly floured surface, roll each half of the dough to about ¼ inch thick.

3. Cut into tree, wreath, star or other shapes with 2½-inch cookie cutters. Place on ungreased cookie sheet. Press candy coated bits into cutouts.

4. Bake 6 to 8 minutes or until edges are firm and bottoms are very lightly browned. Remove from cookie sheet to wire rack. Cool completely.   *About 3½ dozen cookies*

PREP TIME: 30 minutes   **CHILL TIME:** 1 hour
BAKE TIME: 6 minutes

Holiday Bits Cutout Cookies

CHEWY CHOCOLATE MACAROONS

5⅓ cups MOUNDS Sweetened Coconut Flakes
½ cup HERSHEY'S Cocoa
1 can (14 ounces) sweetened condensed milk (not evaporated milk)
2 teaspoons vanilla extract
About 24 red candied cherries, halved (optional)

1. Heat oven to 350°F. Generously grease cookie sheet. Stir together coconut and cocoa in large bowl; stir in sweetened condensed milk and vanilla until well blended. Drop by rounded teaspoons onto prepared cookie sheet. Press cherry half into center of each cookie, if desired.

2. Bake 8 to 10 minutes or until almost set. Immediately remove from cookie sheet to wire rack. Cool completely. Store loosely covered at room temperature. *About 4 dozen cookies*

PREP TIME: 15 minutes   **BAKE TIME:** 8 minutes   **COOL TIME:** 1 hour

CHEWY SKOR TOFFEE BITS COOKIES

2¼ cups all-purpose flour
1 teaspoon baking soda
½ teaspoon salt
½ cup (1 stick) butter or margarine, softened
¾ cup granulated sugar
¾ cup packed light brown sugar
1 teaspoon vanilla extract
2 eggs
1¾ cups (10-ounce package) SKOR English Toffee Bits or 1¾ cups HEATH Bits O' Brickle

1. Heat oven to 350°F. Lightly grease cookie sheet.

2. Stir together flour, baking soda and salt. Beat butter, granulated sugar, brown sugar and vanilla in large bowl until well blended. Add eggs; beat well. Gradually add flour mixture, beating until well blended. Stir in toffee bits. Drop by rounded teaspoons onto prepared cookie sheet.

3. Bake 9 to 11 minutes or until lightly browned. Cool slightly; remove from cookie sheet to wire rack. Cool completely.

About 4 dozen cookies

PREP TIME: 25 minutes   **COOK TIME:** 9 minutes   **COOL TIME:** 1 hour

Chewy Chocolate Macaroons

MINI KISSES COCONUT MACAROON BARS

3¾ cups (10-ounce package) MOUNDS Sweetened
    Coconut Flakes
¾ cup sugar
¼ cup all-purpose flour
¼ teaspoon salt
3 egg whites
1 whole egg, slightly beaten
1 teaspoon almond extract
1 cup HERSHEY'S MINI KISSES Chocolate

1. Heat oven to 350°F. Lightly grease 9-inch square baking pan. Stir together coconut, sugar, flour and salt in large bowl. Add egg whites, whole egg and almond extract; stir until well blended.

2. Stir in MINI KISSES. Spread mixture into prepared pan, covering all chocolate pieces with coconut mixture.

3. Bake 35 minutes or until lightly browned. Cool completely in pan on wire rack. Cover with foil; allow to stand at room temperature about 8 hours or overnight. Cut into bars.   *About 24 bars*

VARIATION: Omit MINI KISSES in batter. Immediately after removing pan from oven, place desired number of chocolate pieces on top, pressing down lightly. Cool completely. Cut into bars.

PREP TIME: 15 minutes   **BAKE TIME:** 35 minutes
COOL TIME: 9 hours

Mini Kisses Coconut Macaroon Bars

PECAN MINI KISSES CUPS

TIP

Use MINI KISSES Chocolate to decorate cakes, cupcakes, cookies and pies. Stir into slightly softened ice cream or sprinkle over top of a sundae for an added chocolate taste treat.

½ cup (1 stick) butter or margarine, softened
1 package (3 ounces) cream cheese, softened
1 cup all-purpose flour
1 egg
⅔ cup packed light brown sugar
1 tablespoon butter, melted
1 teaspoon vanilla extract
  Dash salt
72 HERSHEY'S MINI KISSES Chocolate, divided
½ to ¾ cup coarsely chopped pecans

1. Beat ½ cup softened butter and cream cheese in medium bowl until blended. Add flour; beat well. Cover; refrigerate about 1 hour or until firm enough to handle.

2. Heat oven to 325°F. Stir together egg, brown sugar, 1 tablespoon melted butter, vanilla and salt in small bowl until well blended.

3. Shape chilled dough into 24 balls (1 inch each). Place balls in ungreased small muffin cups (1¾ inches in diameter). Press onto bottom and up side of cups. Place 2 MINI KISSES in each cup. Spoon about 1 teaspoon pecans over chocolate. Fill each cup with egg mixture.

4. Bake 25 minutes or until filling is set. Lightly press 1 MINI KISS into center of each cookie. Cool in pan on wire rack.

24 cups

PREP TIME: 25 minutes   **CHILL TIME:** 1 hour
BAKE TIME: 25 minutes   **COOL TIME:** 1 hour

Pecan Mini Kisses Cups

RICH QUICK & EASY CHOCOLATE BROWNIES

½ **cup sugar**
¼ **cup evaporated milk**
¼ **cup (½ stick) butter or margarine**
8 **bars (8-ounce package) HERSHEY'S Semi-Sweet Baking**
   Chocolate, broken into pieces
2 **eggs**
1 **teaspoon vanilla extract**
¾ **cup all-purpose flour**
¼ **teaspoon baking soda**
¼ **teaspoon salt**
   BROWNIE FROSTING (recipe follows, optional)

1. Heat oven to 325°F. Grease 9-inch square baking pan. Combine sugar, evaporated milk and butter in medium saucepan.

2. Cook over medium heat, stirring constantly, until mixture boils; remove from heat. Add chocolate, stirring until melted. Beat in eggs and vanilla. Stir in flour, baking soda and salt until well blended; pour into prepared pan.

3. Bake 30 to 35 minutes or until brownies just begin to pull away from sides of pan. Cool completely in pan on wire rack. Prepare BROWNIE FROSTING; frost brownies, if desired. Cut into squares.

About 16 brownies

Brownie Frosting

2 **bars (1 ounce each) HERSHEY'S Unsweetened Baking Chocolate,**
   broken into pieces
2 **tablespoons butter or margarine**
1¾ **cups powdered sugar**
⅛ **teaspoon salt**
½ **teaspoon vanilla extract**
2 **to 3 tablespoons water**

Place chocolate and butter in small microwave-safe bowl. Microwave at HIGH (100%) 1 minute; stir. If necessary, microwave an additional 10 seconds at a time, stirring after each heating, just until chocolate is melted when stirred. Combine powdered sugar and salt in medium bowl. Stir in chocolate mixture and vanilla. Add water; beat with spoon to spreading consistency.

About 1 cup frosting

PREP TIME: 30 minutes   **BAKE TIME:** 30 minutes   **COOL TIME:** 2 hours

ULTIMATE CHOCOLATE BROWNIES WITH CREAMY COCOA FROSTING

¾ cup HERSHEY'S Cocoa
½ teaspoon baking soda
⅔ cup butter or margarine, melted and divided
½ cup boiling water
2 cups sugar
2 eggs
1⅓ cups all-purpose flour
1 teaspoon vanilla extract
¼ teaspoon salt
1 cup HERSHEY'S Semi-Sweet Chocolate Chips
CREAMY COCOA FROSTING (recipe follows)

1. Heat oven to 350°F. Grease 13×9×2-inch baking pan. Stir together cocoa and baking soda in large bowl; stir in ⅓ cup butter. Add boiling water; stir until mixture thickens.

2. Stir in sugar, eggs and remaining ⅓ cup butter; stir until smooth. Add flour, vanilla and salt; stir until blended. Stir in chocolate chips. Pour into prepared pan.

3. Bake 35 to 40 minutes or until brownies begin to pull away from sides of pan. Cool completely.

4. Prepare CREAMY COCOA FROSTING; frost brownies. Garnish with additional chips, if desired. Cut into squares.   *About 36 brownies*

Creamy Cocoa Frosting

6 tablespoons butter or margarine, softened
2⅔ cups powdered sugar
½ cup HERSHEY'S Cocoa
¼ cup milk
1 tablespoon espresso powder dissolved in 1 tablespoon hot water
½ teaspoon vanilla extract

Beat butter in medium bowl. Add powdered sugar and cocoa alternately with milk, espresso and vanilla, beating to spreading consistency.

About 2 cups frosting

PREP TIME: 30 minutes   **BAKE TIME:** 35 minutes   **COOL TIME:** 2 hours

HERSHEY'S WHITE CHIP BROWNIES

TIP

Brownies and bar cookies cut into different shapes can add interest to a plate of simple square cookies. Cut cookies into different size rectangles or make triangles by cutting them into 2- to 2½-inch squares; cut each square in half diagonally. To make diamond shapes, cut straight lines 1 or 1½ inches apart the length of the baking pan, then cut straight lines 1½ inches apart diagonally across the pan.

4 eggs
1¼ cups sugar
½ cup (1 stick) butter or margarine, melted
2 teaspoons vanilla extract
1⅓ cups all-purpose flour
⅔ cup HERSHEY'S Cocoa
1 teaspoon baking powder
½ teaspoon salt
1⅔ cups (10-ounce package) HERSHEY'S Premier White Chips

1. Heat oven to 350°F. Grease 13×9×2-inch baking pan. Beat eggs in large bowl until foamy; gradually beat in sugar. Add butter and vanilla; beat until blended.

2. Stir together flour, cocoa, baking powder and salt; add to egg mixture, beating until blended. Stir in white chips. Spread batter into prepared pan.

3. Bake 25 to 30 minutes or until brownies begin to pull away from sides of pan. Cool completely in pan on wire rack. Cut into squares. *About 36 brownies*

PREP TIME: 15 minutes   **BAKE TIME:** 25 minutes
COOL TIME: 2 hours

Hershey's White Chip Brownies

PEANUT BUTTER CHIP TRIANGLES

TIP

To sprinkle powdered sugar over brownies, bars, cupcakes or other desserts, place sugar in a wire mesh strainer. Hold over top of desserts and gently tap sides of strainer.

1½ cups all-purpose flour
½ cup packed light brown sugar
½ cup (1 stick) cold butter or margarine
1⅔ cups (10-ounce package) REESE'S Peanut Butter Chips, divided
1 can (14 ounces) sweetened condensed milk (not evaporated milk)
1 egg, slightly beaten
1 teaspoon vanilla extract
¾ cup chopped walnuts
Powdered sugar (optional)

1. Heat oven to 350°F. Stir together flour and brown sugar in medium bowl. Cut in butter with pastry blender or fork until mixture resembles coarse crumbs. Stir in ½ cup peanut butter chips. Press mixture into bottom of ungreased 13×9×2-inch baking pan. Bake 15 minutes.

2. Meanwhile, in large bowl, combine sweetened condensed milk, egg and vanilla. Stir in remaining chips and walnuts. Spread evenly over hot baked crust.

3. Bake 25 minutes or until golden brown. Cool completely in pan on wire rack. Cut into 2- or 2½-inch squares; cut squares diagonally into triangles. Sift powdered sugar over top, if desired. *24 or 40 triangles*

PREP TIME: 20 minutes   **BAKE TIME:** 40 minutes
COOL TIME: 2 hours

Peanut Butter Chip Triangles

MARBLED CHEESECAKE BARS

CHOCOLATE CRUST (recipe follows)
3 packages (8 ounces each) cream cheese, softened
1 can (14 ounces) sweetened condensed milk (not evaporated milk)
3 eggs
2 teaspoons vanilla extract
2 bars (1 ounce each) HERSHEY'S Unsweetened Baking Chocolate, melted

1. Prepare CHOCOLATE CRUST. Heat oven to 300°F. Beat cream cheese in large bowl until fluffy. Gradually add sweetened condensed milk, beating until smooth. Add eggs and vanilla; mix well.

2. Pour half of batter evenly over prepared crust. Stir melted chocolate into remaining batter; drop by spoonfuls over vanilla batter. With metal spatula or knife, swirl gently through batter to marble.

3. Bake 45 to 50 minutes or until set. Cool in pan on wire rack. Refrigerate several hours until chilled. Cut into bars. Cover; store leftover bars in refrigerator. *24 to 36 bars*

CHOCOLATE CRUST: Stir together 2 cups vanilla wafer crumbs (about 60 wafers), ⅓ cup HERSHEY'S Cocoa and ½ cup powdered sugar. Stir in ½ cup (1 stick) melted butter or margarine until well blended. Press mixture firmly into bottom of ungreased 13×9×2-inch baking pan.

PREP TIME: 25 minutes   **BAKE TIME:** 45 minutes   **COOL TIME:** 1 hour
CHILL TIME: 2½ hours

NUTTY CHOCOLATE BROWNIES

8 bars (8-ounce package) HERSHEY'S Bittersweet Baking Chocolate, broken into pieces
1 cup (2 sticks) butter or margarine
1¼ cups sugar
3 eggs
2 teaspoons vanilla extract
1½ teaspoons powdered instant coffee
1⅓ cups all-purpose flour
½ teaspoon salt
¼ teaspoon baking powder
¼ teaspoon baking soda
1 cup coarsely chopped nuts

1. Heat oven to 350°F. Grease 13×9×2-inch baking pan. Combine chocolate and butter in medium saucepan. Cook over medium heat, stirring constantly, until melted.

2. Remove from heat; stir in sugar. Add eggs, one at a time, stirring well after each addition. Stir in vanilla and instant coffee until blended. Combine flour, salt, baking powder, baking soda and nuts; add to chocolate mixture, stirring until well blended. Spread batter into prepared pan.

3. Bake 25 to 30 minutes or until wooden pick inserted in center comes out almost clean. Cool completely in pan on wire rack. Cut into squares.

About 36 brownies

PREP TIME: 25 minutes   **BAKE TIME:** 25 minutes   **COOL TIME:** 2 hours

MINI KISSES COOKIE BARS

½ **cup (1 stick) butter or margarine, softened**
½ **cup shortening**
1 **cup packed light brown sugar**
½ **cup granulated sugar**
2 **eggs**
1 **teaspoon vanilla extract**
½ **teaspoon baking soda**
2½ **cups all-purpose flour**
1¾ **cups (10-ounce package) HERSHEY'S MINI KISSES Chocolate, divided**
1 **cup chopped nuts (optional)**

1. Heat oven to 375°F. Beat butter and shortening in large bowl on medium speed of mixer just until blended.

2. Add brown sugar and granulated sugar; beat well. Beat in eggs, vanilla and baking soda. Gradually beat in flour (if dough becomes too stiff, stir in remaining flour with spoon). Set aside ½ cup MINI KISSES; stir in remaining MINI KISSES and nuts, if desired. Press dough into ungreased 15½×10½×1-inch jelly-roll pan.

3. Bake 15 to 20 minutes or until top is golden. Remove from oven; immediately place reserved MINI KISSES on top, pressing down lightly. Cool completely in pan on wire rack. Cut into bars.   *About 48 bars*

PREP TIME: 20 minutes   **BAKE TIME:** 15 minutes   **COOL TIME:** 2 hours

MINIATURE BROWNIE CUPS

TIP

Hershey's Dutch Processed Cocoa involves a process which neutralizes the natural acidity found in cocoa powder. This results in a darker cocoa with a more mellow flavor than natural cocoa.

  6 tablespoons butter or margarine, melted
¾ cup sugar
½ teaspoon vanilla extract
  2 eggs
½ cup all-purpose flour
¼ cup HERSHEY'S Cocoa or HERSHEY'S Dutch
    Processed Cocoa
¼ teaspoon baking powder
   Dash salt
¼ cup finely chopped nuts

1. Heat oven to 350°F. Line small muffin cups (1¾ inches in diameter) with paper bake cups. Stir together butter, sugar and vanilla in medium bowl. Add eggs; beat well with spoon.

2. Stir together flour, cocoa, baking powder and salt; gradually add to butter mixture, beating with spoon until well blended. Fill muffin cups ½ full with batter; sprinkle nuts over top.

3. Bake 12 to 15 minutes or until wooden pick inserted in center comes out almost clean. Cool slightly; remove brownies from pan to wire rack. Cool completely.

About 24 brownies

PREP TIME: 20 minutes **BAKE TIME:** 12 minutes
COOL TIME: 25 minutes

Miniature Brownie Cups

MARBLED CHERRY BROWNIES

CHERRY CREAM FILLING (recipe follows)
½ cup (1 stick) butter or margarine, melted
⅓ cup HERSHEY'S Cocoa
 2 eggs
 1 cup sugar
 1 teaspoon vanilla extract
½ cup all-purpose flour
½ teaspoon baking powder
¼ teaspoon salt

1. Prepare CHERRY CREAM FILLING; set aside. Heat oven to 350°F. Grease 9-inch square baking pan. Stir butter and cocoa in small bowl until well blended; cool slightly.

2. Beat eggs in medium bowl until foamy. Gradually add sugar and vanilla, beating until well blended. Stir together flour, baking powder and salt; add to egg mixture. Add cocoa mixture; stir until well blended.

3. Spread half of chocolate batter into prepared pan; cover with cherry filling. Drop spoonfuls of remaining chocolate batter over filling. With knife or spatula, gently swirl chocolate batter into filling for marbled effect.

4. Bake 35 to 40 minutes or until brownies begin to pull away from sides of pan. Cool; cut into squares. Cover; refrigerate leftover brownies. Bring to room temperature to serve.   *About 16 brownies*

Cherry Cream Filling

 1 package (3 ounces) cream cheese, softened,
¼ cup sugar
 1 egg
½ teaspoon vanilla extract
¼ teaspoon almond extract
⅓ cup chopped maraschino cherries, well drained
 1 to 2 drops red food color (optional)

1. Beat cream cheese and sugar in small bowl on medium speed of electric mixer until blended. Add egg, vanilla and almond extract; beat well. (Mixture will be thin.)

2. Stir in cherries and food color, if desired.

PREP TIME: 25 minutes   **BAKE TIME:** 35 minutes   **COOL TIME:** 1½ hours

Marbled Cherry Brownies

CREAMY DOUBLE DECKER FUDGE

1 cup REESE'S Peanut Butter Chips
1 can (14 ounces) sweetened condensed milk
   (not evaporated milk), divided
1 teaspoon vanilla extract, divided
1 cup HERSHEY'S Semi-Sweet Chocolate Chips

1. Line 8-inch square pan with foil, extending foil over edges of pan. Place peanut butter chips and ⅔ cup sweetened condensed milk in small microwave-safe bowl.

2. Microwave at HIGH (100%) 1 to 1½ minutes, stirring after 1 minute, until chips are melted and mixture is smooth when stirred. Stir in ½ teaspoon vanilla; spread evenly into prepared pan.

3. Place remaining sweetened condensed milk and chocolate chips in another small microwave-safe bowl; repeat above microwave procedure. Stir in remaining ½ teaspoon vanilla; spread evenly over peanut butter layer. Cover; refrigerate until firm. Remove from pan; place on cutting board. Peel off foil. Cut into squares. Store, tightly covered, in refrigerator.

About 4 dozen pieces or 1½ pounds

NOTE: For best results, do not double this recipe.

PREP TIME: 15 minutes   **COOK TIME:** 3 minutes
CHILL TIME: 2 hours

Creamy Double Decker Fudge

RICH COCOA FUDGE

    3 cups sugar
    ⅔ cup HERSHEY'S Cocoa or HERSHEY'S Dutch Processed Cocoa
    ⅛ teaspoon salt
1½ cups milk
    ¼ cup (½ stick) butter
    1 teaspoon vanilla extract

1. Line 8- or 9-inch square pan with foil, extending foil over edges of pan. Butter foil.

2. Stir together sugar, cocoa and salt in heavy 4-quart saucepan; stir in milk. Cook over medium heat, stirring constantly, until mixture comes to full rolling boil. Boil, without stirring, until mixture reaches 234°F on candy thermometer or until small amount of mixture dropped into very cold water, forms a soft ball which flattens when removed from water. (Bulb of candy thermometer should not rest on bottom of saucepan.) Remove from heat.

3. Add butter and vanilla. DO NOT STIR. Cool at room temperature to 110°F (lukewarm). Beat with wooden spoon until fudge thickens and just begins to lose some of its gloss. Quickly spread into prepared pan; cool completely. Cut into squares. Store in tightly covered container at room temperature.   *About 3 dozen pieces or 1¾ pounds*

NOTE: For best results, do not double this recipe.

NUTTY RICH COCOA FUDGE: Beat cooked fudge as directed. Immediately stir in 1 cup chopped almonds, pecans or walnuts and quickly spread into prepared pan.

MARSHMALLOW-NUT COCOA FUDGE: Increase cocoa to ¾ cup. Cook fudge as directed. Add 1 cup marshmallow creme with butter and vanilla. DO NOT STIR. Cool to 110°F (lukewarm). Beat 8 minutes; stir in 1 cup chopped nuts. Pour into prepared pan. (Fudge does not set until poured into pan.)

PREP TIME: 25 minutes   **COOK TIME:** 25 minutes   **COOL TIME:** 2½ hours

CHOCOLATE PEANUT CLUSTERS

½ cup HERSHEY'S Milk Chocolate Chips
½ cup HERSHEY'S Semi-Sweet Chocolate Chips
 1 tablespoon shortening (do not use butter, margarine or oil)
 1 cup unsalted, roasted peanuts

1. Place milk chocolate chips, semi-sweet chocolate chips and shortening in small microwave-safe bowl. Microwave at HIGH (100%) 1 to 1½ minutes or just until chips are melted and mixture is smooth when stirred. Stir in peanuts.

2. Drop by teaspoons into 1-inch diameter candy or petit four papers. Allow to set until firm. Store in airtight container in cool, dry place.

About 2 dozen candies

PREP TIME: 15 minutes   **COOK TIME:** 1 minute   **COOL TIME:** 1 hour

FOOLPROOF DARK CHOCOLATE FUDGE

 3 cups (1½ packages, 12-ounces each) HERSHEY'S Semi-Sweet
    Chocolate Chips
 1 can (14 ounces) sweetened condensed milk (not evaporated milk)
    Dash salt
 1 cup chopped walnuts
1½ teaspoons vanilla extract

1. Line 8- or 9-inch square pan with foil, extending foil over edges of pan. Melt chocolate chips with sweetened condensed milk and salt in heavy saucepan over low heat. Remove from heat; stir in walnuts and vanilla. Spread evenly into prepared pan.

2. Refrigerate 2 hours or until firm. Remove from pan; place on cutting board. Peel off foil; cut into squares. Store loosely covered at room temperature. *About 5 dozen pieces or 2 pounds*

NOTE: For best results, do not double this recipe.

PREP TIME: 10 minutes   **COOK TIME:** 15 minutes   **CHILL TIME:** 2 hours

CASHEW MACADAMIA CRUNCH

          2 cups (11.5 ounce package) HERSHEY'S Milk Chocolate Chips
        ¾ cup coarsely chopped salted or unsalted cashews
        ¾ cup coarsely chopped salted or unsalted macadamia nuts
        ½ cup (1 stick) butter, softened
        ½ cup sugar
          2 tablespoons light corn syrup

1. Line 9-inch square pan with foil, extending foil over edges of pan. Butter foil. Cover bottom of prepared pan with chocolate chips.

2. Combine cashews, macadamia nuts, butter, sugar and corn syrup in large heavy skillet; cook over low heat, stirring constantly, until butter is melted and sugar is dissolved. Increase heat to medium; cook, stirring constantly, until mixture begins to cling together and turns golden brown.

3. Pour mixture over chocolate chips in pan, spreading evenly. Cool. Refrigerate until chocolate is firm. Remove from pan; peel off foil. Break into pieces. Store, tightly covered in cool, dry place.   *About 1½ pounds*

PREP TIME: 30 minutes   **COOK TIME:** 10 minutes   **COOL TIME:** 40 minutes
CHILL TIME: 3 hours

CHOCOLATE & PEANUT BUTTER TRUFFLES

        ¾ cup (1½ sticks) butter (no substitutes)
          1 cup REESE'S Peanut Butter Chips
        ½ cup HERSHEY'S Cocoa
          1 can (14 ounces) sweetened condensed milk (not evaporated milk)
          1 tablespoon vanilla extract
            HERSHEY'S Cocoa or finely chopped nuts or graham cracker
              crumbs

1. Melt butter and peanut butter chips in saucepan over very low heat. Add cocoa; stir until smooth. Add sweetened condensed milk; stir constantly until mixture is thick and glossy, about 4 minutes. Remove from heat; stir in vanilla.

2. Refrigerate 2 hours or until firm enough to handle. Shape into 1-inch balls; roll in cocoa. Refrigerate until firm, about 1 hour. Store, covered, in refrigerator.   *About 3½ dozen candies*

PREP TIME: 30 minutes   **COOK TIME:** 7 minutes   **CHILL TIME:** 3 hours

Cashew Macadamia Crunch

OLD–FASHIONED CREAMY FUDGE

2 cups sugar
¾ cup milk
2½ bars (1 ounce each) HERSHEY'S Unsweetened Baking Chocolate,
     broken into pieces
2 tablespoons light corn syrup
¼ teaspoon salt
2 tablespoons butter
1 teaspoon vanilla extract

1. Line 8-inch square pan with foil, extending foil over edges of pan. Lightly butter foil.

2. Stir together sugar, milk, baking chocolate, corn syrup and salt in heavy 2-quart saucepan. Cook over medium heat, stirring constantly, until mixture comes to full rolling boil. Cook, stirring occasionally, until mixture reaches 234°F on candy thermometer or until small amount of mixture dropped into very cold water forms a soft ball, which flattens when removed from water. (Bulb of candy thermometer should not rest on bottom of saucepan.)

3. Remove from heat. Add butter and vanilla. DO NOT STIR. Cool at room temperature to 110°F (lukewarm). Beat with wooden spoon until fudge thickens and just begins to lose some of its gloss. Quickly spread into prepared pan. Cool completely. Cut into squares. Store in tightly covered container at room temperature.

About 3 dozen pieces or 1½ pounds

NOTE: For best results, do not double this recipe.

PREP TIME: 20 minutes   **COOK TIME:** 25 minutes   **COOL TIME:** 2½ hours

WHITE COATED CHOCOLATE TRUFFLES

½ cup whipping cream
3 tablespoons butter
1 cup HERSHEY'S Semi-Sweet Chocolate Chips
1 teaspoon vanilla extract
   WHITE COATING (page 59)

1. Combine whipping cream and butter in medium saucepan. Cook over medium heat, stirring constantly, just until mixture begins to boil; remove from heat. Add chocolate chips, stirring until completely melted;

continue stirring until mixture cools and thickens slightly. Stir in vanilla. Pour into shallow, glass dish. Cover; refrigerate until firm.

2. To form truffles, with spoon, scoop mixture; shape into 1-inch balls. Place on wax paper-lined tray. Cover; refrigerate until firm. Prepare WHITE COATING. Dip truffles into coating; refrigerate. Serve well chilled. Store in tightly covered container in refrigerator.

About 2 dozen truffles

WHITE COATING: Combine 1⅔ cups (10-ounce package) HERSHEY'S Premier White Chips with 1 tablespoon shortening (do not use butter, margarine or oil) in small microwave-safe bowl. Microwave at HIGH (100%) 1 minute or just until chips are melted when stirred. (Coating works best for dipping between 85° and 90°F. If coating goes below 85°F, place bowl in larger bowl containing warm water; stir until temperature reaches 85°F. Be careful not to get any water into coating mixture.)

PREP TIME: 1 hour   **COOK TIME:** 3 minutes   **COOL TIME:** 10 minutes
CHILL TIME: 5 hours

CHOCOLATE CHIP PEANUT BUTTER FUDGE

      4 cups sugar
      1 jar (7 ounces) marshmallow creme
  1½ cups (12-ounce can) evaporated milk
      1 cup REESE'S Creamy or Crunchy Peanut Butter
      1 tablespoon butter or margarine
      1 cup HERSHEY'S Semi-Sweet Chocolate Chips or HERSHEY'S
          Milk Chocolate Chips

1. Line 13×9×2-inch pan with foil, extending foil over edges of pan. Lightly butter foil.

2. Stir together sugar, marshmallow creme, evaporated milk, peanut butter and butter in heavy 4-quart saucepan. Cook over medium heat, stirring constantly, until mixture comes to full rolling boil; boil and stir 5 minutes. Remove from heat. Immediately add chocolate chips, stir until smooth. Pour into prepared pan; cool until firm.

3. Use foil to lift fudge out of pan; peel off foil. Cut fudge into squares. Store in tightly covered container in cool, dry place.

About 8 dozen pieces or 3½ pounds

NOTE: For best results, do not double this recipe.

PREP TIME: 15 minutes   **COOK TIME:** 15 minutes   **COOL TIME:** 3 hours

CHOCOLATE–COVERED ALMOND APRICOT TASSIES

TIP

When melting chocolate, even a small amount of moisture my cause it to "seize" or become stiff and grainy. Chocolate can sometimes be returned to melting consistency by adding 1 teaspoon solid shortening (do not use butter, margarine or oil) for every 2 ounces of chocolate and reheating it.

2 cups vanilla wafer crumbs (about 60 wafers, crushed)
1 cup finely chopped almonds
⅓ cup HERSHEY'S Cocoa
1 can (14 ounces) sweetened condensed milk (not evaporated milk)
1 package (8 ounces) dried apricots, chopped
½ cup chopped candied cherries
¼ teaspoon almond extract
2 cups (11.5-ounce package) HERSHEY'S Milk Chocolate Chips
4 teaspoons shortening

1. Line small muffin cups (1¾ inches in diameter) with paper bake cups.

2. Combine crumbs, almonds and cocoa in large bowl. Add sweetened condensed milk, apricots, cherries and almond extract; mix well. Refrigerate 30 minutes. Roll mixture into 1-inch balls; press into prepared muffin cups.

3. Place chocolate chips and shortening in medium microwave-safe bowl. Microwave at HIGH (100%) 1½ minutes; stir. If necessary, microwave at HIGH an additional 15 seconds at a time, stirring after each heating, just until chips are melted when stirred. Spoon about 1 teaspoon melted chocolate over each filled cup. Refrigerate until chocolate is set. Store, covered, in refrigerator.

About 6 dozen candies

PREP TIME: 40 minutes   **COOK TIME:** 1½ minutes
CHILL TIME: 1 hour

Chocolate-Covered Almond Apricot Tassies

CHOCOLATE COCONUT BALLS

    3 bars (1 ounce each) HERSHEY'S Unsweetened Baking Chocolate
¼ cup (½ stick) butter
½ cup sweetened condensed milk (not evaporated milk)
¾ cup granulated sugar
¼ cup water
    1 tablespoon light corn syrup
    1 teaspoon vanilla extract
    2 cups MOUNDS Sweetened Coconut Flakes
    1 cup chopped nuts
        Powdered sugar

1. Melt chocolate and butter in large heavy saucepan over very low heat. Add sweetened condensed milk; stir to blend. Remove from heat.

2. Stir together granulated sugar, water and corn syrup in small saucepan. Cook over medium heat, stirring constantly, until sugar is dissolved. Cook, without stirring, until mixture reaches 250°F on candy thermometer or until a small amount of syrup, when dropped into very cold water, forms a firm ball which does not flatten when removed from water. (Bulb of candy thermometer should not rest on bottom of saucepan.) Remove from heat; stir into chocolate mixture. Add vanilla, coconut and nuts; stir until well blended.

3. Refrigerate about 30 minutes or until firm enough to handle. Shape into 1-inch balls; roll in powdered sugar. Store tightly covered in cool, dry place.   *About 4 dozen candies*

NOTE: For best results, do not double this recipe.

PREP TIME: 25 minutes   **COOK TIME:** 20 minutes   **CHILL TIME:** 30 minutes

HERSHEY'S BUCKEYES

¾ cup (1½ sticks) butter or margarine, softened
1⅓ cups REESE'S Crunchy Peanut Butter
    3 cups powdered sugar
    2 cups (12-ounce package) HERSHEY'S Semi-Sweet Chocolate
        Chips
    1 tablespoon shortening (do not use butter, margarine or oil)

1. Beat butter and peanut butter in large bowl until blended. Gradually add powdered sugar, beating until well blended. Cover; refrigerate until firm enough to shape, about 30 minutes.

2. Shape into 1-inch balls. Cover; refrigerate until firm, about 1 hour.

3. Place chocolate chips and shortening in medium microwave-safe bowl. Microwave at HIGH (100%) 1½ minutes; stir. If necessary, microwave at HIGH an additional 15 seconds at a time, stirring after each heating, just until chips are melted when stirred.

4. Dip each ball into chocolate mixture, coating ¾ of ball. Place on wax paper, uncoated side up. Let stand until chocolate hardens. Store, covered, in refrigerator.   *About 5 dozen candies*

PREP TIME: 30 minutes   **CHILL TIME:** 1½ hours   **COOK TIME:** 1½ minutes
COOL TIME: 1 hour

QUICK HOLIDAY RASPBERRY FUDGE

3⅓ cups (two 10-ounce packages) HERSHEY'S Raspberry Chips or
3⅓ cups HERSHEY'S Semi-Sweet Chocolate Chips
1 can (14 ounces) sweetened condensed milk (not evaporated milk)
1½ teaspoons vanilla extract or raspberry-flavored liqueur

1. Line 8-inch square pan with foil, extending foil over edges of pan.

2. Place raspberry chips and sweetened condensed milk in medium microwave-safe bowl. Microwave at HIGH (100%) 1 minute; stir. If necessary, microwave an additional 30 seconds at a time, stirring after each heating, just until chips are melted and mixture is smooth when stirred; stir in vanilla. Spread evenly into prepared pan.

3. Cover; refrigerate 2 hours or until firm. Remove from pan; place on cutting board. Peel off foil; cut into squares. Store loosely covered at room temperature.   *About 4 dozen pieces or 2 pounds*

NOTE: For best results, do not double this recipe.

PREP TIME: 5 minutes   **COOK TIME:** 1 minute   **CHILL TIME:** 2 hours

CHOCOLATEY MOCHA CREME

- 1 package (6-serving size, about 5 ounces) chocolate cook & serve pudding and pie filling mix*
- 2 tablespoons powdered instant espresso
- 3 cups skim milk
- 2 cups (12-ounce package) HERSHEY'S Reduced Fat Semi-Sweet Baking Chips
- ½ cup frozen light non-dairy whipped topping, thawed HERSHEY'S Cocoa

Do not use instant pudding mix.

1. Stir pudding mix and instant espresso into milk in medium saucepan. Cook over medium heat, stirring constantly, until mixture comes to full boil; remove from heat. Add chips; stir until chips are melted and mixture is smooth. Spoon into small dessert dishes.

2. Press plastic wrap directly onto surface. Serve slightly warm or chilled. Garnish each with 1 tablespoon whipped topping. Dust with cocoa.   *8 servings*

PREP TIME: 20 minutes   **CHILL TIME:** 3 hours

NUTRITIONAL INFORMATION PER SERVING: ½ Cup
290 Calories (60 Calories from Fat), 7 g Total Fat* (11% Daily Value), 6 g Saturated Fat* (30% Daily Value), 0 mg Cholesterol (0% Daily Value), 120 mg Sodium (5% Daily Value), 51 g Total Carbohydrate (17% Daily Value), 3 g Dietary Fiber (12% Daily Value), 41 g Sugars, 6 g Protein, 2% Daily Value Vitamin A, 0% Daily Value Vitamin C, 120 mg Calcium (10% Daily Value) 6% Daily Value Iron

Fat content adjusted for reduced availability of fat from Salatrim.

Chocolatey Mocha Creme

SUNNY COCOA DROP COOKIES

½ cup (1 stick) 60% vegetable oil spread
⅔ cup granulated sugar
⅔ cup lowfat sour cream
 1 egg white
 1 teaspoon vanilla extract
¼ teaspoon freshly grated orange peel
1¾ cups all-purpose flour
 3 tablespoons HERSHEY'S Cocoa
 1 teaspoon baking soda
½ teaspoon baking powder
¼ teaspoon ground cinnamon
   COCOA GLAZE (recipe follows)

1. Heat oven to 350°F. Spray cookie sheet with vegetable cooking spray.

2. Beat vegetable oil spread and granulated sugar in large bowl on medium speed of electric mixer until light and fluffy. Add sour cream, egg white, vanilla and orange peel; beat until well blended. Stir together flour, cocoa, baking soda, baking powder and cinnamon; gradually add to sugar mixture, beating until blended. Drop dough by rounded teaspoons onto prepared cookie sheet.

3. Bake 10 to 12 minutes or until set. Remove from cookie sheet to wire rack. Cool completely. Prepare COCOA GLAZE; drizzle over tops of cookies. Store, covered, at room temperature.   *4 dozen cookies*

Cocoa Glaze

 1 tablespoon 60% vegetable oil spread
 2 tablespoons water
 1 tablespoon HERSHEY'S Cocoa
½ cup powdered sugar
½ teaspoon vanilla extract

Melt vegetable oil spread in small saucepan over low heat. Stir in water and cocoa. Cook, stirring constantly, until thick. Do not boil. Remove from heat; gradually add powdered sugar and vanilla, beating with spoon or whisk to drizzling consistency.   *About ⅓ cup glaze*

PREP TIME: 30 minutes   **BAKE TIME:** 10 minutes

NUTRITIONAL INFORMATION PER SERVING: 2 Cookies
100 Calories (35 Calories from Fat), 4 g Total Fat (6% Daily Value), 1 g Saturated Fat
(5% Daily Value), <5 mg Cholesterol (1% Daily Value), 125 mg Sodium (5% Daily Value),
16 g Total Carbohydrate (5% Daily Value), <1 g Dietary Fiber (2% Daily Value), 9 g Sugars,
1 g Protein, 4% Daily Value Vitamin A, 0% Daily Value Vitamin C, 0% Daily Value Calcium,
2% Daily Value Iron

REDUCED FAT CHOCOLATEY SAUCE

        2 cups (12-ounce package) HERSHEY'S Reduced Fat Semi-Sweet
           Baking Chips
        1 cup lowfat evaporated milk
       ⅓ cup sugar
     1½ teaspoons vanilla extract
           Frozen yogurt or ice cream

1. Place chips and evaporated milk in medium microwave-safe bowl.
Microwave at HIGH (100%) 4 to 5 minutes, stirring after each minute of
heating, until chips are melted and smooth.

2. Add sugar and vanilla; beat with whisk until well blended. Cool
slightly. Serve over frozen yogurt or ice cream. Cover; refrigerate leftover
sauce.   *About 2 cups sauce*

NOTE: To reheat sauce, place in small microwave-safe bowl. Microwave at
HIGH 1 to 1½ minutes or until desired temperature

PREP TIME: 3 minutes   **COOK TIME:** 4 minutes   **COOL TIME:** 10 minutes

NUTRITIONAL INFORMATION PER SERVING: 2 Tablespoons
90 Calories (25 Calories from Fat), 2.5 g Total Fat* (4% Daily Value), 2 g Saturated Fat*
(20% Daily Value), 0 mg Cholesterol (0% Daily Value), 0 mg Sodium (0% Daily Value),
15 g Total Carbohydrate (5% Daily Value), <1 g Dietary Fiber (4% Daily Value), 13 g Sugars,
2 g Protein, 0% Daily Value Vitamin A, 0% Daily Value Vitamin C, 25 mg Calcium
(2% Daily Value), 6% Daily Value Iron

Fat content adjusted for reduced availability of fat from Salatrim.

CRUNCHY–TOPPED COFFEE CAKE WITH CHOCOLATEY CHIPS

1⅓ cups all-purpose flour
½ cup packed light brown sugar
¼ cup granulated sugar
½ teaspoon baking soda
¼ teaspoon baking powder
⅓ cup 60% vegetable oil spread, softened
½ cup buttermilk or sour milk*
¼ cup frozen egg substitute, thawed
1 cup HERSHEY'S Reduced Fat Semi-Sweet Baking Chips, divided
2 tablespoons finely chopped walnuts
Frozen light non-dairy whipped topping, thawed (optional)
Sliced strawberries (optional)

*To sour milk: Use 1½ teaspoons white vinegar plus milk to equal ½ cup.

1. Heat oven to 350°F. Spray 9-inch round baking pan with vegetable cooking spray.

2. Stir together flour, brown sugar, granulated sugar, baking soda and baking powder in large bowl. Cut in spread until crumbly; reserve ½ cup mixture for topping. Stir together buttermilk and egg substitute; add to remaining crumb mixture, stirring until well blended. Spread batter into prepared pan. Sprinkle ¾ cup chips on top. Stir together reserved crumbs, remaining ¼ cup chips and walnuts; sprinkle on top.

3. Bake 25 to 30 minutes or until wooden pick inserted near center comes out clean. Cool in pan on wire rack. Cut into wedges; serve with dollop of whipped topping and sliced strawberries, if desired.   *8 servings*

PREP TIME: 20 minutes   **BAKE TIME:** 25 minutes   **COOL TIME:** 1½ hours

NUTRITIONAL INFORMATION PER SERVING: 1 Piece
320 Calories (90 Calories from Fat), 10 g Total Fat* (15% Daily Value), 4 g Saturated Fat* (20% Daily Value), 0 mg Cholesterol (0% Daily Value), 170 mg Sodium (8% Daily Value), 52 g Total Carbohydrate (17% Daily Value), 2 g Dietary Fiber (8% Daily Value), 33 g Sugars, 5 g Protein, 10% Daily Value Vitamin A, 0% Daily Value Vitamin C, 50 mg Calcium (4% Daily Value) 10% Daily Value Iron

Fat content adjusted for reduced availability of fat from Salatrim.

Crunchy-Topped Coffee Cake with Chocolatey Chips

ELEGANT CHOCOLATE ANGEL TORTE

⅓ cup HERSHEY'S Cocoa
1 package (about 15 ounces) "two-step" angel food cake mix
2 envelopes (1.3 ounces each) dry whipped topping mix
1 cup cold skim milk
1 teaspoon vanilla extract
1 cup strawberry purée*
Strawberries

Mash 2 cups sliced fresh strawberries (or frozen berries, thawed) in blender or food processor. Cover; blend until smooth. Purée should measure 1 cup.

1. Move oven rack to lowest position. Sift cocoa over contents of cake flour packet; stir to blend. Proceed with mixing cake as directed on package. Bake and cool as directed for 10-inch tube pan. Carefully run knife along side of pan to loosen cake; remove from pan. Using serrated knife, slice cake horizontally into four layers.

2. Prepare whipped topping mix as directed on package, using 1 cup milk and 1 teaspoon vanilla. Blend in strawberry purée. Place bottom cake layer on serving plate; spread with ¼ of topping. Set next cake layer on top; spread with ¼ of topping. Continue layering cake and topping. Garnish with strawberries. Refrigerate until ready to serve. Slice cake with sharp serrated knife, cutting with gentle sawing motion. Cover; refrigerate leftover cake.   *About 16 servings*

PREP TIME: 30 minutes   **BAKE TIME:** 45 minutes   **COOL TIME:** 2 hours

NUTRITIONAL INFORMATION PER SERVING: 1 Piece
150 Calories (20 Calories from Fat), 2 g Total Fat (3% Daily Value), 2 g Saturated Fat (10% Daily Value), 0 mg Cholesterol (0% Daily Value), 210 mg Sodium (9% Daily Value), 28 g Total Carbohydrate (9% Daily Value), 1 g Dietary Fiber (4% Daily Value), 22 g Sugars, 4 g Protein, 0% Daily Value Vitamin A, 20% Daily Value Vitamin C, 50 mg Calcium (4% Daily Value), 2% Daily Value Iron

Elegant Chocolate Angel Torte

HERSHEY'S 50% REDUCED FAT CHOCOLATEY CHIP COOKIES

2¼ cups all-purpose flour
1 teaspoon baking soda
½ teaspoon salt
½ cup (1 stick) 60% vegetable oil spread
¾ cup granulated sugar
¾ cup packed light brown sugar
1 teaspoon vanilla extract
2 eggs
2 cups (12-ounce package) HERSHEY'S Reduced Fat Semi-Sweet Baking Chips

1. Heat oven to 375°F. Stir together flour, baking soda and salt in medium bowl.

2. Beat spread, granulated sugar, brown sugar and vanilla in large bowl with electric mixer until creamy. Add eggs; beat well. Gradually add flour mixture, beating well. Stir in chips. Drop by rounded teaspoons onto ungreased cookie sheet.

3. Bake 8 to 10 minutes or until lightly browned. Cool slightly; remove from cookie sheet to wire rack.

5 dozen cookies

NOTE: To make softer, chewier cookies, add 1 or 2 tablespoons unsweetened applesauce to egg mixture.

PAN RECIPE: Spray 15½×10½×1-inch jelly-roll pan with vegetable cooking spray; spread batter into pan. Bake at 375°F 18 to 20 minutes or until lightly browned. Cool completely; cut into bars. *About 60 bars*

CHOCOLATE CHOCOLATEY CHIP COOKIES: Add ⅓ cup HERSHEY'S Cocoa to flour mixture; follow directions above for mixing and baking.

PREP TIME: 25 minutes   **BAKE TIME:** 8 minutes

NUTRITIONAL INFORMATION PER SERVING: 1 Cookie
70 Calories (20 Calories from Fat), 2 g Total Fat* (3% Daily Value), 1 g Saturated Fat* (5% Daily Value), 5 mg Cholesterol (2% Daily Value), 60 mg Sodium (3% Daily Value), 13 g Total Carbohydrate (4% Daily Value), <1 g Dietary Fiber (3% Daily Value), 9 g Sugars, 1 g Protein, 0% Daily Value Vitamin A, 0% Daily Value Vitamin C, 0% Daily Value Calcium, 0% Daily Value Iron

Fat content adjusted for reduced availability of fat from Salatrim. 2 g of fat per serving vs. 4.5 g in regular HERSHEY'S CLASSIC CHOCOLATE CHIP COOKIE.

QUICK CHOCOLATE CUPCAKES

1½ cups all-purpose flour
¾ cup sugar
¼ cup HERSHEY'S Cocoa
1 teaspoon baking soda
½ teaspoon salt
1 cup water
¼ cup vegetable oil
1 tablespoon white vinegar
1 teaspoon vanilla extract
Powdered sugar (optional)

1. Heat oven to 375°F. Line muffin cups (2½ inches in diameter) with paper bake cups.

2. Stir together flour, sugar, cocoa, baking soda and salt in medium bowl. Add water, oil, vinegar and vanilla; beat with whisk just until batter is smooth and ingredients are well blended. Fill muffin cups ⅔ full with batter.

3. Bake 16 to 18 minutes or until wooden pick inserted in center comes out clean. Remove from pan to wire rack. Cool completely. Sift with powdered sugar, if desired.

16 cupcakes

PREP TIME: 10 minutes   **BAKE TIME:** 16 minutes   **COOL TIME:** 1 hour

NUTRITIONAL INFORMATION PER SERVING: 1 Cupcake
110 Calories (30 Calories from Fat), 3.5 g Total Fat (5% Daily Value), 0.5 g Saturated Fat (3% Daily Value), 0 mg Cholesterol (0% Daily Value), 150 mg Sodium (6% Daily Value), 19 g Total Carbohydrate (6% Daily Value), <1 g Dietary Fiber (3% Daily Value), 10 g Sugars, 1 g Protein, 0% Daily Value Vitamin A, 0% Daily Value Vitamin C, 0% Daily Value Calcium, 4% Daily Value Iron

HERSHEY'S 50% REDUCED FAT CHOCOLATE SWIRLED CHEESEPIE

1 carton (8 ounces) lowfat vanilla yogurt
½ cup graham cracker crumbs
1 package (8 ounces) Neufchâtel cheese (⅓ less fat), softened
½ cup sugar
¾ teaspoon vanilla extract
2 eggs
1 cup HERSHEY'S Reduced Fat Semi-Sweet Baking Chips
⅓ cup HERSHEY'S Syrup (do not use Lite Syrup)

1. Line rust-proof colander with cheesecloth or large coffee filter; place colander over bowl. Spoon yogurt into prepared colander; drain 1 to 2 hours. Remove yogurt from cheesecloth; discard liquid.

2. Heat oven to 350°F. Lightly spray 9-inch pie plate with vegetable cooking spray. Sprinkle graham cracker crumbs on bottom of plate.

3. Beat Neufchâtel cheese, sugar and vanilla on medium speed of electric mixer until well blended. Add yogurt; beat well. Add eggs; beat well. Place chips and syrup in small microwave-safe bowl. Microwave at HIGH (100%) 45 seconds; stir until chips are melted. Gradually add ¾ cup cheese mixture, stirring until well blended. Alternately spoon vanilla and chocolate mixtures into prepared pan (chocolate will be thicker). Using knife, swirl for marbled effect.

4. Bake 30 to 35 minutes or until center is almost set. Cool. Refrigerate about 4 hours before serving.   *8 to 10 servings*

PREP TIME: 2¼ hours   **BAKE TIME:** 30 minutes   **COOL TIME:** 1 hour
CHILL TIME: 4 hours

NUTRITIONAL INFORMATION PER SERVING: 1 Piece

260 Calories (90 Calories from Fat), 10 g Total Fat* (15% Daily Value), 6 g Saturated Fat* (30% Daily Value), 60 mg Cholesterol (20% Daily Value), 160 mg Sodium (7% Daily Value), 37 g Total Carbohydrate (12% Daily Value), 1 g Dietary Fiber (4% Daily Value), 31 g Sugars, 6 g Protein, 6% Daily Value Vitamin A, 0% Daily Value Vitamin C, 6% Daily Value Calcium, 4% Daily Value Iron

Fat content adjusted for reduced availability of fat from Salatrim. 10 g of fat per serving vs. 22 g in regular CHOCOLATE SWIRLED CHEESEPIE.

Hershey's 50% Reduced Fat Chocolate Swirled Cheesepie

EASY CHOCOLATE LOVER'S CHEESEPIE

3 packages (8 ounces each) cream cheese, softened
¾ cup sugar
3 eggs
1 teaspoon vanilla extract
2 cups (12-ounce package) HERSHEY'S MINICHIPS Semi-Sweet Chocolate, divided
1 extra serving-size packaged graham cracker crumb crust (9 ounces)
2 tablespoons whipping cream

1. Heat oven to 450°F. Beat cream cheese and sugar with electric mixer in large bowl until well blended. Add eggs and vanilla; beat well. Stir in 1⅔ cups small chocolate chips; pour into crust.

2. Bake 10 minutes. Without opening oven door, reduce temperature to 250°F; continue baking 30 minutes or just until set.

3. Remove from oven to wire rack. Cool completely. Cover; refrigerate until thoroughly chilled.

4. Place remaining ⅓ cup chips and whipping cream in small microwave-safe bowl.

5. Microwave at HIGH (100%) 20 to 30 seconds or just until chips are melted and mixture is smooth when stirred. Cool slightly; spread over top of cheesepie. Refrigerate 15 minutes or until topping is set. Cover; refrigerate leftover cheesepie.   *10 servings*

PREP TIME: 15 minutes   **BAKE TIME:** 40 minutes
COOL TIME: 1 hour   **CHILL TIME:** 4 hours

Easy Chocolate Lover's Cheesepie

EASY CHOCOLATE CREAM–FILLED TORTE

1 frozen pound cake (10¾ ounces), thawed
½ cup powdered sugar
¼ cup HERSHEY'S Cocoa
1 cup (½ pint) cold whipping cream
1 teaspoon vanilla extract
   CHOCOLATE GLAZE (recipe follows)
   Sliced almonds (optional)

1. Cut cake horizontally to make 4 layers. Stir together sugar and cocoa in medium bowl. Add whipping cream and vanilla; beat until stiff.

2. Place bottom cake layer on serving platter. Spread ⅓ of the whipped cream mixture on cake layer. Place next cake layer on top of whipped cream; continue layering whipped cream mixture and cake until all have been used.

3. Prepare CHOCOLATE GLAZE; spoon over top of cake, allowing to drizzle down sides. Garnish with almonds, if desired. Refrigerate until ready to serve. Cover; refrigerate leftover torte.   *8 to 10 servings*

Chocolate Glaze

2 tablespoons butter or margarine
2 tablespoons HERSHEY'S Cocoa
2 tablespoons water
1 cup powdered sugar
¼ to ½ teaspoon almond extract

1. Melt butter in small saucepan over low heat. Add cocoa and water. Cook, stirring constantly, until smooth and slightly thickened. Do not boil.

2. Remove from heat. Gradually add powdered sugar and almond extract, beating with whisk until smooth.   *About ½ cup glaze*

PREP TIME: 20 minutes   **CHILL TIME:** 30 minutes

Easy Chocolate Cream-Filled Torte

COCOA CAPPUCCINO MOUSSE

1 can (14 ounces) sweetened condensed milk (not evaporated milk)
⅓ cup HERSHEY'S Cocoa
3 tablespoons butter or margarine
2 teaspoons powdered instant coffee or espresso, dissolved in
    2 teaspoons hot water
2 cups (1 pint) cold whipping cream

1. Combine sweetened condensed milk, cocoa, butter and coffee in medium saucepan. Cook over low heat, stirring constantly, until butter melts and mixture is smooth. Remove from heat; cool.

2. Beat whipping cream in large bowl until stiff. Gradually fold chocolate mixture into whipped cream. Spoon into dessert dishes. Refrigerate until set, about 2 hours. Garnish as desired. *8 servings*

PREP TIME: 15 minutes   **COOK TIME:** 10 minutes   **CHILL TIME:** 2 hours

CHOCOLATE CHEESEPIE

1 package (8 ounces) cream cheese, softened
1 package (3 ounces) cream cheese, softened
¾ cup sugar
1 teaspoon vanilla extract
¼ cup HERSHEY'S Cocoa
2 eggs
½ cup whipping cream
1 packaged graham cracker crumb crust (6 ounces)
    Cherry pie or peach pie filling or sliced fresh fruit

1. Heat oven to 350°F. Beat cream cheese, sugar and vanilla in large bowl until well blended.

2. Add cocoa; beat until well blended; scraping sides of bowl and beaters frequently. Add eggs; beat well. Stir in whipping cream. Pour into crust.

3. Bake 35 to 40 minutes. (Center will be soft but will set upon cooling.) Cool to room temperature. Cover; refrigerate several hours or overnight. Serve with pie filling. Cover; refrigerate leftover pie. *6 to 8 servings*

PREP TIME: 10 minutes   **BAKE TIME:** 35 minutes   **CHILL TIME:** 4 to 6 hours

Cocoa Cappuccino Mousse

CHOCOLATE CHERRY CREAM–FILLED LOG

    4 eggs, separated
  ½ cup granulated sugar
    1 teaspoon vanilla extract
  ⅓ cup granulated sugar
  ⅓ cup HERSHEY'S Cocoa
  ½ cup all-purpose flour
  ¼ teaspoon baking powder
  ¼ teaspoon baking soda
  ⅛ teaspoon salt
  ⅓ cup water
    Powdered sugar
    1 can (21 ounces) cherry pie filling, divided
1½ cups whipped topping
    CHOCOLATE GLAZE (recipe page 84)

1. Heat oven to 375°F. Line 15½×10½×1/2-inch jelly-roll pan with foil; generously grease foil.

2. Beat egg whites in large bowl until foamy; gradually add ½ cup granulated sugar, beating until stiff peaks form.

3. Beat egg yolks and vanilla in small bowl on high speed for about 3 minutes. Gradually add ⅓ cup granulated sugar; continue beating 2 minutes. Combine cocoa, flour, baking powder, baking soda and salt; add to egg yolk mixture alternately with water on low speed, beating just until batter is smooth.

4. Fold chocolate mixture gradually into egg whites; spread evenly in prepared pan.

5. Bake 12 to 15 minutes or until top springs back when touched lightly in center. Immediately loosen cake from edges of pan; invert on towel sprinkled with powdered sugar. Carefully remove foil. Immediately roll cake in towel starting from narrow end; place on wire rack to cool.

6. Combine 1 cup pie filling and whipped topping, mix well. Unroll cake; remove towel. Spread with filling; reroll cake.

7. Prepare CHOCOLATE GLAZE; drizzle over top, allowing to run down sides of cake. Refrigerate several hours. Just before serving, spoon ½ cup pie filling over cake. Serve with remaining pie filling.   *10 to 12 servings*

(continued on page 84)

Chocolate Cherry Cream-Filled Log

(Chocolate Cherry Cream-Filled Log, continued)

Chocolate Glaze

2 tablespoons butter or margarine
2 tablespoons HERSHEY'S Cocoa
2 tablespoons water
1 cup powdered sugar
½ teaspoon vanilla extract

1. Melt butter in small saucepan over low heat. Add cocoa and water. Cook, stirring constantly, until smooth and slightly thickened. Do not boil.

2. Remove from heat; cool slightly. Gradually blend in sugar and vanilla.

PREP TIME: 30 minutes   **BAKE TIME:** 12 minutes   **COOL TIME:** 1 hour
CHILL TIME: 3 hours

HOT FUDGE PUDDING CAKE

1¼ cups granulated sugar, divided
1 cup all-purpose flour
7 tablespoons HERSHEY'S Cocoa, divided
2 teaspoons baking powder
¼ teaspoon salt
½ cup milk
⅓ cup butter or margarine, melted
1½ teaspoons vanilla extract
½ cup packed light brown sugar
1¼ cups hot water
Whipped topping

1. Heat oven to 350°F. Stir together ¾ cup granulated sugar, flour, 3 tablespoons cocoa, baking powder and salt. Stir in milk, butter and vanilla; beat until smooth.

2. Pour batter into ungreased 9-inch square baking pan. Stir together remaining ½ cup granulated sugar, brown sugar and remaining 4 tablespoons cocoa; sprinkle mixture evenly over batter. Pour hot water over top. Do not stir.

3. Bake 35 to 40 minutes or until center is almost set. Let stand 15 minutes; spoon into dessert dishes, spooning sauce from bottom of pan over top. Garnish with whipped topping.   *About 8 servings*

PREP TIME: 10 minutes   **BAKE TIME:** 35 minutes   **COOL TIME:** 15 minutes

BITTERSWEET TRUFFLE TOFFEE MOUSSE PIE

1¾ cups (10-ounce package) SKOR English Toffee Bits or 1¾ cups
    HEATH Bits 'O Brickle, divided
1 tablespoon water
1 package (8 ounces) cream cheese, softened
4 bars (1 ounce each) HERSHEY'S Bittersweet Baking Chocolate,
    divided
1 cup (½ pint) cold whipping cream, divided
1 baked (9 inch) pie crust, cooled
½ teaspoon shortening (do not use butter, margarine or oil)

1. Combine 1 cup toffee bits and water in small saucepan. Cook over medium heat, stirring constantly, until toffee is melted. Gradually beat toffee mixture into cream cheese in medium bowl. Refrigerate 20 minutes.

2. Place 3 ounces chocolate and 3 tablespoons whipping cream in small microwave-safe bowl. Microwave at HIGH (100%) 1 minute; stir. If necessary, microwave an additional 15 seconds or until chocolate is melted and mixture is smooth when stirred. Spread chocolate mixture onto bottom of baked crust; refrigerate.

3. Beat remaining whipping cream in small bowl until stiff; gradually stir into toffee mixture, mixing thoroughly. Gently stir in ½ cup bits. Spread over chocolate layer. Cover; refrigerate until well chilled, about 3 hours.

4. Shortly before serving, place remaining 1 bar of chocolate and shortening in small microwave bowl. Microwave at HIGH 1 minute or until chocolate is melted and smooth when stirred; drizzle over top of pie. Garnish with remaining ¼ cup toffee bits. Refrigerate until drizzle is set. Cover; refrigerate leftover pie. *6 to 8 servings*

PREP TIME: 30 minutes   **COOK TIME:** 12 minutes   **CHILL TIME:** 3½ hours

ITALIAN RICOTTA TORTE

....

  8 eggs, separated
1½ cups sugar, divided
1½ cups ground blanched almonds
  ⅔ cup all-purpose flour
  ⅔ cup HERSHEY'S Cocoa
  1 teaspoon baking soda
  ½ teaspoon salt
  ½ cup water
  2 teaspoons vanilla extract
  ½ teaspoon almond extract
    RICOTTA CHERRY FILLING (recipe page 88)
    COCOA WHIPPED CREAM (recipe page 88)
    Candied cherries or sliced almonds (optional)

1. Heat oven to 375°F. Grease bottoms of two 9-inch round baking pans; line with wax paper. Grease wax paper lining leaving sides of pans ungreased.

2. Beat egg yolks in large bowl on medium speed of electric mixer 3 minutes. Gradually add 1 cup sugar, beating another 2 minutes. Stir together almonds, flour, cocoa, baking soda and salt; add alternately with water to egg yolk mixture, beating on low speed just until blended. Stir in vanilla and almond extract.

3. Beat egg whites in large bowl until foamy. Gradually add remaining ½ cup sugar, beating until stiff peaks form. Carefully fold chocolate mixture into beaten egg whites. Spread batter evenly into prepared pans.

4. Bake 20 to 22 minutes or until top springs back when touched lightly. Cool 10 minutes; remove from pans to wire racks. Cool completely. With long serrated knife, cut each layer in half horizontally to make 4 thin layers. Refrigerate layers while preparing filling and whipped cream.

5. Place one cake layer on serving plate; spread with ⅓ (about 1⅓ cups) RICOTTA CHERRY FILLING. Top with another cake layer. Repeat with remaining filling and cake layers. Frost sides and top of torte with COCOA WHIPPED CREAM. Garnish with candied cherries or almonds, if desired. Refrigerate at least 4 hours. Cover; refrigerate leftover torte.

8 to 10 servings

(continued on page 88)

Italian Ricotta Torte

(Italian Ricotta Torte, continued)

Ricotta Cherry Filling

1 cup (½ pint) cold whipping cream
1¾ cups (15 ounces) ricotta cheese
⅓ cup powdered sugar
½ cup chopped candied cherries
½ teaspoon almond extract

1. Beat whipping cream in small bowl until stiff. Beat ricotta cheese and powdered sugar in large bowl until smooth.

2. Fold whipped cream into cheese mixture just until blended. Stir in candied cherries and almond extract.   *About 4 cups filling*

COCOA WHIPPED CREAM: Stir together ⅔ cup powdered sugar and ⅓ cup HERSHEY'S Cocoa in large bowl. Add 2 cups (1 pint) cold whipping cream and 2 teaspoons vanilla extract; beat just until stiff. (Do not overbeat.)   *About 4 cups*

PREP TIME: 40 minutes   **BAKE TIME:** 20 minutes   **COOL TIME:** 1 hour
CHILL TIME: 4 hours

MINI CHOCOLATE PIES

1 package (4-serving size) chocolate cook & serve pudding and pie
   filling mix*
1 cup HERSHEY'S MINICHIPS Semi-Sweet Chocolate
1 package (4 ounces) single serve graham cracker crusts (6 crusts)
   Whipped topping
   Additional MINICHIPS Semi-Sweet Chocolate

Do not use instant pudding mix.

1. Prepare pudding and pie filling mix as directed on package; remove from heat. Immediately add 1 cup small chocolate chips; stir until melted. Cool 5 minutes, stirring occasionally.

2. Pour filling into crusts; press plastic wrap directly onto surface. Refrigerate several hours or until firm. Garnish with whipped topping and small chocolate chips.   *6 servings*

PREP TIME: 5 minutes   **COOK TIME:** 10 minutes   **COOL TIME:** 5 minutes
CHILL TIME: 2 hours

Mini Chocolate Pies

PEANUT BUTTER ICE CREAM SAUCE

1⅔ cups (10-ounce package) REESE'S Peanut Butter Chips
½ cup evaporated milk
3 tablespoons light corn syrup
1 tablespoon butter or margarine
1½ teaspoons vanilla extract

1. Stir together peanut butter chips, evaporated milk, corn syrup and butter in small microwave-safe bowl.

2. Microwave at HIGH (100%) 1 to 1½ minutes or until chips are melted and mixture is smooth when stirred. If necessary, microwave an additional 30 seconds at a time, stirring after each heating, just until mixture is smooth when stirred. Stir in vanilla. Serve warm over ice cream.   *About 1½ cups sauce*

PREP TIME: 2 minutes   **COOK TIME:** 1 minute   **COOL TIME:** 10 minutes

EUROPEAN FUDGE SAUCE

¾ cup HERSHEY'S Dutch Processed Cocoa
¾ cup granulated sugar
½ cup packed light brown sugar
   Dash salt
¾ cup whipping cream
½ cup (1 stick) butter, softened
1 teaspoon vanilla extract
½ cup toasted nuts, coarsely chopped* (optional)

*To toast nuts: Heat oven 350°F. Spread nuts in thin layer in shallow baking pan. Bake 8 to 10 minutes, stirring occasionally, until light golden brown; cool.

1. Combine cocoa, granulated sugar, brown sugar and salt in medium saucepan. Stir in whipping cream and butter. Cook over medium heat, stirring constantly, until mixture comes to a boil.

2. Remove from heat; let stand 5 minutes. Stir in vanilla and nuts, if desired. Serve warm over cake, ice cream or other desserts.
                                          About 2 cups sauce

PREP TIME: 5 minutes   **COOK TIME:** 8 minutes   **COOL TIME:** 10 minutes

Top to bottom: Peanut Butter Ice Cream Sauce, SKOR Bits Sauce (page 92), European Fudge Sauce

SKOR BITS SAUCE

1¾ cups (10-ounce package) SKOR English Toffee Bits or
    1¾ cups HEATH Bits 'O Brickle
½ cup whipping cream
2 tablespoons light corn syrup
2 tablespoons butter
    Vanilla ice cream

1. Stir together toffee bits, whipping cream and corn syrup in small saucepan.

2. Cook over medium heat, stirring constantly, until mixture comes to a boil. Remove from heat.

3. Add butter; stir until melted. Cool. Serve over ice cream.

About 1⅔ cups sauce

PREP TIME: 2 minutes   **COOK TIME:** 10 minutes   **COOL TIME:** 20 minutes

REESE'S PEANUT BUTTER 'N' CHOCOLATE PIE

1⅓ cups HERSHEY'S MINI KISSES Chocolate, divided
2 tablespoons milk
1 packaged crumb crust (6 ounces)
1 package (8 ounces) Neufchâtel cheese (⅓ less fat), softened
¾ cup sugar
1 cup REESE'S Creamy or Crunchy Peanut Butter
3½ cups (8 ounces) frozen non-dairy whipped topping, thawed

1. Place ⅔ cup MINI KISSES and milk in small microwave-safe bowl . Microwave at HIGH (100%) 30 to 45 seconds or just until melted and smooth when stirred; spread evenly onto bottom of crust. Cover; refrigerate.

2. Beat Neufchâtel cheese in medium bowl until smooth; gradually beat in sugar. Stir in peanut butter and whipped topping until blended; spoon evenly into crust over chocolate mixture. Cover; refrigerate until set, at least 4 hours.

3. Place remaining ⅔ cup chocolate pieces around edge of filling just before serving. Serve cold; cover and refrigerate leftover pie.

8 servings

PREP TIME: 20 minutes   **COOK TIME:** 30 seconds   **CHILL TIME:** 4 hours

Bar Cookies
Marbled Cheesecake
Bars, 46
Mini Kisses Coconut
Macaroon Bars, 36
Mini Kisses Cookie Bars,
47
Peanut Butter Chip
Triangles, 44
Bittersweet Truffle Toffee
Mousse Pie, 85
Broiled Topping, 16
Brownie Frosting, 40
Brownies
Hershey's White Chip
Brownies, 42
Marbled Cherry
Brownies, 50
Miniature Brownie
Cups, 48
Nutty Chocolate Brownies,
46
Rich Quick & Easy
Chocolate Brownies, 40
Ultimate Chocolate
Brownies with Creamy
Cocoa Frosting, 41

Cakes & Cheesecakes
Chocolate Cherry Cream-
Filled Log, 82
Chocolate Raspberry
Pound Cake, 12
Chocolatetown Special
Cake, 10
Chocolate Truffle Cake
Supreme, 11
Crunchy-Topped Cocoa
Cake, 16
Crunchy-Topped Coffee
Cake with Chocolatey
Chips, 68
Deep Dark Chocolate
Cake, 15
Easy Chocolate Cream-
Filled Torte, 78
Elegant Chocolate Angel
Torte, 70
Fudge Truffle Cheesecake,
20
Hot Fudge Pudding
Cake, 84
Italian Ricotta Torte, 86
Peanut Butter Chip
Cheesecake, 10
Quick 'n' Easy Chocolate
Cupcakes, 14
Quick Chocolate
Cupcakes, 73

Take-Me-to-a-Picnic
Cake, 18
Toffee Bits Cheesecake, 8
Candy
Cashew Macadamia
Crunch, 56
Chocolate & Peanut Butter
Truffles, 56
Chocolate Coconut
Balls, 62
Chocolate-Covered
Almond Apricot Tassies,
60
Chocolate Peanut Clusters,
55
Hershey's Buckeyes, 62
White Coated Chocolate
Truffles, 58
Cashew Macadamia
Crunch, 56
Cherry Cream Filling, 50
Chewy Chocolate Macaroons,
34
Chocolate Almond Biscotti,
28
Chocolate & Peanut Butter
Truffles, 56
Chocolate Cheesepie, 80
Chocolate Cherry Cream-
Filled Log, 82
Chocolate Chip Peanut Butter
Fudge, 59
Chocolate Chocolatey Chip
Cookies, 72
Chocolate Coconut Balls, 62
Chocolate-Covered Almond
Apricot Tassies, 60
Chocolate Crumb Crust, 8, 20
Chocolate Crust, 46
Chocolate Garnish, 18
Chocolate Glaze, 28, 78, 84
Chocolate Haystacks, 30
Chocolate Peanut Clusters, 55
Chocolate Raspberry Pound
Cake, 12
Chocolatetown Special
Cake, 10
Chocolate Truffle Cake
Supreme, 11
Chocolatey Mocha Creme, 64
Cocoa Cappuccino
Mousse, 80
Cocoa Glaze, 66
Cocoa Whipped Cream, 88
Coconut and Pecan
Filling, 26
Cookies
Chewy Chocolate
Macaroons, 34

Chocolate Almond
Biscotti, 28
Chocolate Chocolatey Chip
Cookies, 72
Chocolate Haystacks, 30
Fudgey Cocoa No-Bake
Treats, 24
Fudgey German Chocolate
Sandwich Cookies, 26
Hershey's Chocolatetown
Chip Cookies, 30
Hershey's 50% Reduced
Fat Chocolatey Chip
Cookies, 72
Hershey's Mini Kisses
Chocolate Blossoms, 25
Hershey's Mini Kisses
Peanut Blossoms, 24
Holiday Bits Cutout
Cookies, 32
Holiday Chocolate
Shortbread Cookies, 22
No-Bake Butterscotch
Haystacks, 30
Pecan Mini Kisses Cups, 38
Skor Bits & Chocolate Chip
Cookies, 31
Sunny Cocoa Drop
Cookies, 66
Creamy Cocoa Frosting, 41
Creamy Double Decker
Fudge, 52
Creamy Fudge Frosting, 14
Crunchy-Topped Cocoa
Cake, 16
Crunchy-Topped Coffee Cake
with Chocolatey Chips,
68
Crusts
Chocolate Crumb Crust,
4, 20
Chocolate Crust, 46

Deep Dark Chocolate Cake, 15

Easy Chocolate Cream-Filled
Torte, 78
Easy Chocolate Lover's
Cheesepie, 76
Elegant Chocolate Angel
Torte, 70
European Fudge Sauce, 90

Fillings
Cherry Cream Filling, 50
Coconut and Pecan
Filling, 26
Raspberry Cream, 12
Ricotta Cherry Filling, 88

Foolproof Dark Chocolate Fudge, 55
Frostings
Brownie Frosting, 40
Creamy Cocoa Frosting, 41
Creamy Fudge Frosting, 14
One-Bowl Buttercream Frosting, 15
Peanut Butter Chip Frosting, 18
Fudge
Chocolate Chip Peanut Butter Fudge, 59
Creamy Double Decker Fudge, 52
Foolproof Dark Chocolate Fudge, 55
Marshmallow-Nut Cocoa Fudge, 54
Nutty Rich Cocoa Fudge, 54
Old-Fashioned Creamy Fudge, 58
Quick Holiday Raspberry Fudge, 63
Rich Cocoa Fudge, 54
Fudge Truffle Cheesecake, 20
Fudgey Cocoa No-Bake Treats, 24
Fudgey German Chocolate Sandwich Cookies, 26

Glazes
Chocolate Glaze, 28, 78, 84
Cocoa Glaze, 66
White Coating, 59
White Glaze, 28

Hershey's Buckeyes, 62
Hershey's Chocolatetown Chip Cookies, 30
Hershey's 50% Reduced Fat Chocolate Swirled Cheesepie, 74
Hershey's 50% Reduced Fat Chocolatey Chip Cookies, 72
Hershey's Mini Kisses Chocolate Blossoms, 25
Hershey's Mini Kisses Peanut Blossoms, 24
Hershey's White Chip Brownies, 42
Holiday Bits Cutout Cookies, 32
Holiday Chocolate Shortbread Cookies, 22
Hot Fudge Pudding Cake, 84

Italian Ricotta Torte, 86

Marbled Cheesecake Bars, 46
Marbled Cherry Brownies, 50
Marshmallow-Nut Cocoa Fudge, 54
Miniature Brownie Cups, 48
Mini Chocolate Pies, 88
Mini Kisses Coconut Macaroon Bars, 36
Mini Kiss Cookie Bars, 47

No-Bake Butterscotch Haystacks, 30
Nutty Chocolate Brownies, 46
Nutty Rich Cocoa Fudge, 54

Old-Fashioned Creamy Fudge, 58
One-Bowl Buttercream Frosting, 15

Peanut Butter Chip Cheesecake, 10
Peanut Butter Chip Frosting, 18
Peanut Butter Chip Triangles, 44
Peanut Butter Ice Cream Sauce, 90
Pecan Mini Kisses Cups, 38
Pies
Bittersweet Truffle Toffee Mousse Pie, 85
Chocolate Cheesepie, 80
Easy Chocolate Lover's Cheesepie, 76
Hershey's 50% Reduced Fat Chocolate Swirled Cheesepie, 74
Mini Chocolate Pies, 88
Reese's Peanut Butter 'n' Chocolate Pie, 92

Quick 'n' Easy Chocolate Cupcakes, 14
Quick Chocolate Cupcakes, 73
Quick Holiday Raspberry Fudge, 63

Raspberry Cream, 12
Reduced Fat Chocolatey Sauce, 67
Reese's Peanut Butter 'n' Chocolate Pie, 92
Rich Cocoa Fudge, 56
Rich Quick & Easy Chocolate Brownies, 40

Ricotta Cherry Filling, 88

Sauces
European Fudge Sauce, 90
Peanut Butter Ice Cream Sauce, 90
Reduced Fat Chocolatey Sauce, 67
Skor Bits Sauce, 92
Skor Bits & Chocolate Chip Cookies, 31
Skor Bits Sauce, 92
Sunny Cocoa Drop Cookies, 66

Take-Me-to-a-Picnic Cake, 18
Toffee Bits Cheesecake, 8
Toppings
Broiled Topping, 16
Chocolate Garnish, 18
Cocoa Whipped Cream, 88

Ultimate Chocolate Brownies with Creamy Cocoa Frosting, 41

White Coated Chocolate Truffles, 58
White Coating, 59
White Glaze, 28